Antique Radio Restoration Guide

Wallace-Homestead Book Company
Radnor, Pennsylvania

Second Edition

Antique Radio Restoration Guide

David Johnson

Published in Radnor, Pennsylvania 19089,
by Wallace-Homestead,
a division of Chilton Book Company

Designed by Arlene Putterman
Manufactured in the United States of America

Library of Congress Cataloging in Publication Data
Johnson, David, 1933–
    Antique radio restoration guide / David Johnson.
        p.   cm.
    Rev. ed. of: Antique radios. c1982.
    Includes index.
    ISBN 0-87069-638-6
    1. Radio—Receivers and reception—Collectors
and collecting. 2. Radio—Receivers and
reception—Conservation and restoration.
I. Johnson, David, 1933–   Antique radios.
II. Title.
TK6563.J57   1992
621.384′187—dc20   92-50193
                                                          CIP

1 2 3 4 5 6 7 8 9 0   1 0 9 8 7 6 5 4 3 2

This volume is dedicated
to all the designers and engineers,
known and unknown,
who developed the technology
that has made modern communications possible.
May we who work with their old equipment
appreciate their genius.

Contents

Acknowledgments

Many minds and sources contribute to a book like this. It distills personal experience and combines it with the tips and experience of many other service people. In gathering all this together, a new generation can enjoy the rewards of keeping and maintaining old electronic equipment.

I especially want to acknowledge McGraw-Hill Publishing Company for permission to use illustrations from the John Markus book entitled *Television and Radio Repairing*. A special thank-you goes to Bob Howe for scanning the text for the original manuscript onto a computer disk so I did not have to key all of it again. I also want to thank Virgil Byng for much-needed advice on the photography for the book.

Finally, I would like to acknowledge the growing number of collectors and restorers of old radios who have made a second edition of this book necessary. I hope it will be useful to all who read it.

David Johnson

Antique Radio Restoration Guide

Introduction

In the years since the first edition of *Antique Radio Restoration Guide* (as *Antique Radios: Restoration and Price Guide*) was published in 1982, many thousands of new collectors have entered the field. At that time about half a dozen books on the subject of antique radios were in print and only two, including this one, on restoration.

Now there are dozens of books covering all facets of the radio collection and restoration field. There are price guides that track the changes in popularity (and therefore the price) of collectible receivers. Some highly desirable radios have prices in the five-figure range.

But there is plenty of room at the entry level for those who just enjoy working with their bit of electronics history, and hundreds of thousands of common old sets are still out there to challenge the new collector.

This book is intended for the person who is just getting started in collecting and restoring. It will take the new collector through the early steps of selecting a radio, cleaning it and examining it, testing it, and bringing it back to a useful and satisfying life.

For the investment of $100 in equipment and another $100 in parts and interesting low-priced radios, the new collector can enjoy many months of learning and the satisfaction of bringing an old set back to life!

This book is a beginner's book. There are other, more advanced books on the market, and many more techniques and ideas than can be contained in one book. As you become more experienced, you will want other books, both new and old, on servicing.

This book also is concerned with safe servicing—handling potentially dangerous radios in a safe way so that neither the radio nor the service person are damaged. This edition has a whole new chapter, entitled Safety Precautions; read it carefully.

How to Use This Book

Before you start working on any radio, even before you buy one, read the first six chapters. Understand them thoroughly so that you can intelligently examine an old radio.

Before spending money on supplies or test equipment, read the last chapter (Your Electronics Shop). Don't buy more equipment than you need. You already probably will have some of the tools. It is good to buy as the need arises.

Once you get an old radio and know its condition, refer to the chapters on troubleshooting (Chapter 7) and repair (Chapter 8) to fix it. Some of the other books on servicing will have ideas that can aid you as well.

Once you have the radio running, you can fine-tune it and repair the cabinet.

The chapter on receiver theory (Chapter 11) will help you understand what happens electronically inside that set. Use it when you get confused in your troubleshooting. In understanding *how* the receiver works, you nearly always can find out *why* it doesn't work. Chapter 11 is a chapter you will read many times.

The Appendix will guide you in identifying common tubes.

Above all, take your time and have fun. You are learning something new, and you are preserving an important piece of history, electronics history.

1 Choosing an Antique Radio

There are many reasons why people begin to collect and restore old radios. Maybe they were given an old set or found one in an attic, or they might have taken a fancy to one they saw at a garage sale or auction. No matter how an antique radio is found, its new owner will want to make it attractive and useable.

It's not difficult to improve the appearance of an old radio, and often it isn't hard to make it work well. But to do both, collectors will have to do some work and use their heads. This book contains tips and basic technical information about restoring old radio sets. You, the collector, will have to supply the work and the thinking. If you are confused by terms in this chapter, use the Glossary in the back of this book or move on to the short course in electronics and radio function in Chapter 2.

Acquiring an antique radio is a personal decision. You must want the set you see. Ask yourself questions like these when you first see a prospect: *Would I enjoy having and using it?*; *Does it bring back memories of one I knew when I was younger?*; *Is it particularly handsome or unusual?*; *Do I think I can fix it?*

For information on what various sets are worth, in general and in particular, there are a number of price guides available (among them *Guide to Old Radios: Pointers, Pictures and Prices* by David and Betty Johnson, Wallace-Homestead, 1989). Any price guide is only approximate. The most important question is *What is it worth to me?*

One warning is in order here. Watch out! Collecting and fixing radios can be habit-forming, as the author of this book so well knows.

Determining Age

This section is only a rough guide on determining age.

Primitive radios. The earliest sets (circa 1920 to 1922) were often homemade, using only one or two tubes or no tubes at all. No attempt was made to make them pretty. They have historical value to the advanced collector but are not much fun for the beginner. Of course, if someone gives you one, don't throw it away!

Classical radios. Manufactured from about 1922 to 1928, classical radios were the first of the home entertainment receivers. Frequently they have many dials and are almost always battery powered. They use tube types like '01A, '12A, and '71A. They often have interesting cabinets. These radios are quite rare and may be expensive. Since they are battery powered and the correct batteries no longer are made or are hard to find, they will usually need to have power supplies built for them.

Mass-market sets. These were made from about 1929 through 1946. During this period there was a nearly complete changeover to superheterodyne receivers and AC power sources. Their electronics were sometimes complex. The only battery sets produced were portables and farm radios. Sets made during this era often have wooden cabinets, many of which are very fancy, but plastic cabinets also came into extensive use during this period.

Designed with EXTRAS... to sell that EXTRA set!!

FADA

5 EXQUISITE COLORS TO MATCH ANY COLOR SCHEME IN THE HOME OR OFFICE!

Illustrated are two of the new exciting line of 1946 FADA Table Models. Beautifully designed in 5 scintillating colors, these FADA radio receivers provide those "extras" that make your customers anxious to buy more than one.

FADA extra sales mean extra profits!

FADA *Sensive-Tone*

FADA 6 tube models are equipped with the new FADA "Sensive-Tone" ... assuring greater sensitivity and clearer reception.

652 SERIES

6 Tube A.C.-D.C. Superheterodynes with the R.F. Noise Reducing Stage with Slide Rule Dial in Gemlike "FADA-LUCENT" Cabinets.

6 tube radio with 8 tube performance. Features include the new Lock in type tubes; Beam Power Output System; New Wonder Speaker ALNICO V; Automatic Volume Control and FADA-SCOPE built-in LOOP ANTENNA. Housed in beautiful "FADA-LUCENT" Cabinets in Five Gorgeous COLOR COMBINATIONS resembling precious stones.

1000 SERIES

6 Tube A.C.-D.C. Superheterodynes ... In Gemlike "FADA-LUCENT" Cabinets with the New Gemloid Illuminated Dial and Noise Reducing R.F. Stage.

8 tube performance with 6 full working tubes; FADA-SCOPE built-in loop ANTENNA; Beam Power Output System; Automatic Volume Control; New Wonder Speaker ALNICO V. Housed in beautiful "FADA-LUCENT" Cabinets in Five Gorgeous COLOR COMBINATIONS resembling precious stones.

YOU CAN ALWAYS DEPEND ON

FADA *Radio*

Famous Since Broadcasting Began!

FADA RADIO AND ELECTRIC COMPANY, INC., LONG ISLAND CITY, N. Y.

Fada 1946 models 1000 and 652. These Catalin sets are electronically conventional (six-tube AC/DC) but are today highly collectible and expensive. This ad is from Radio News, *May 1946.*

Capehart 1953 model TC101 gray plastic five-tube AC/DC radio.

Dictograph circa 1920s intercom desk unit. Such odd electrical equipment can add interest to a collection.

Pilot 1947 model T-601 five-tube AC design FM tuner, designed to plug into the phonograph input on a radio. This early high-band tuner came in a wooden case.

They have become collectible in their own right, and some of them are very expensive. These radios are fun to collect and use and often can be bought for a reasonable price.

Postwar radios. These sets, made from about 1947 through 1960, are generating a good deal of interest. Plastic cabinets prevail, and the wooden ones are undistinguished. Most radios of this era are now inexpensive and easy to fix. They will become more collectible as time goes on. These are good radios with which to get acquainted as you develop your restoring skills.

Solid-state sets. These radios, manufactured from about 1961 to the present, use transistors and integrated circuits rather than tubes. They are not discussed in this book. They are becoming collectible, however, especially the unusual-looking ones.

What Kind of Power?

Your radio will need one of three types of power, depending sometimes on the set's age. The first type is battery power, which was used in older radios. These radios can be identified by a bundle of wires emerging to join a multiple-connection plug or metal lugs. While these sets are rather simple, they often require battery designs that are no longer available. A power pack must be built for these sets in order to run them from a household AC line. For this reason, they aren't the best sets for beginners.

Other battery radios are the traditional portables, usually identified by their luggage-type cases. Many of these will operate on AC power as well.

The second type, the AC set, is probably the one with which you will want to start. When these sets are fixed, they are very usable. They can be identified by the line cord and plug, of course, and are usually quite heavy because they have a power transformer and chokes in the power supply. They have their own special problems for restorers but are still the best starting place for beginners.

The third type is a special kind of AC set, the AC/DC receiver. This set has a line cord and plug but is usually much lighter in weight because it has no power transformer. These less-expensive sets frequently have plastic cabinets. They are very satisfactory to use. They can be easy to work on but are, under certain conditions, highly dangerous. Never test one outside its cabinet without reading Problems of AC/DC Receivers in Chapter 7.

Determining Condition

You cannot thoroughly examine a radio until you get it home, but before you buy you can estimate its condition. Some problem signs will affect your decision to buy and the price you'll pay.

Disasters

Cabinet in poor condition with large pieces of veneer or wood missing. There may be water damage to the veneer, and the wooden speaker grille may be broken with pieces missing. Small veneer problems can be solved, and some separation of veneer into layers can be repaired with glue. Likewise, broken grilles with the wooden pieces still on hand can be glued. You can do a lot with a cabinet, but not everything. Broken plastic cabinets fit into the same class. Don't bother with them unless you need the parts.

Radio chassis burned and blackened. Either the power supply has burned up or the set has been hit by lightning. The damage is usually too severe to repair.

Radio chassis badly rusted. Along with cabinet water damage, this usually indicates that the set has been in water. Probably too many parts have been ruined to try fixing this set.

Possible Disasters

Extreme mouse damage. Many of the visible wires have been chewed, and it may look as if mice actually have been nesting in the radio. Some mouse damage can be fixed, but too much of it makes the set not worth the trouble. I once picked up a set from a farmer and, upon looking into the back, saw two small eyes looking at me. I shook the set a few times and left it outside for a few minutes so its occupant could leave. The set repaired nicely and works fine.

Major parts missing. Some parts can be replaced but others, built for a particular set or model, may be hard to find. This set requires a judgment call. You must decide if you want to

All the Magic of FM

with the New DELCO RADIO Combination

LET IT storm and thunder! In any weather, at any time of the day or night, FM reception over the new Delco Console Combination is amazingly static-free. Always, the programs are magically clear—perfectly reproduced.

There are scores of good, solid engineering reasons for the thrilling performance of the new Delco Combination. It has 14 tubes plus rectifier, with three short-wave bands in addition to AM and FM . . . a big 15-inch speaker for finer reproduction . . . a tone control providing 12 different bass and treble combinations . . . and many more advanced features.

The record player features a special lightweight tone arm with *jeweled-point* pick-up, and handles fourteen 10-inch or ten 12-inch records. It rides smoothly in and out on a ball-bearing roller mechanism, and shuts off automatically after the last record plays.

PUSH-BUTTON TUNING FOR FM, TOO! The new Delco Console Combination provides *push-button* tuning for *both* AM and FM.

Exquisite workmanship and unusual distinction of design mark the 18th-century cabinets. Two models are available: R-1251 in walnut, and R-1252 in mahogany—both masterpieces of fine furniture.

To see and hear *the best of all that's new in radio,* ask your United Motors Service distributor to demonstrate the new Delco Combination and other popular Delco radio models.

DELCO RADIO
A GENERAL MOTORS PRODUCT

Delco radios are distributed nationally by United Motors Service. See your United Motors distributor about the Delco radio line.

Delco 1947 FM/AM console advertisement in Radio News, *June 1947.*

The Crown Princess

*S*atin walnut finish accented by an edge-lighted dial gives this new Air King radio-phonograph a beauty of appearance equalled only by the purity and naturalness of its tone. Styled with simple dignity, it fits naturally into any decorative scheme. Engineered by Air King, it wins the enthusiasm of the critical musician. And, produced by Air King, its quality demands no penalty of price.

Features that make the Crown Princess a superlative instrument include:

Six tube (including rectifier) superheterodyne for standard broadcast. Two dual-purpose tubes give eight-tube reception. AC or DC. Automatic changer for ten- or twelve-inch records. Permanent Alnico No. 5 magnet speaker. Featherweight, low-pressure tone arm. Permanent needle. Crystal pick-up. Automatic volume control. Full range tone control. Beam power output. Built-in loop aerial.

The Royalty of Radio Since 1920

AIR KING
RADIO
Brooklyn

Division of
HYTRON RADIO & ELECTRONICS CORPORATION

The Royal Family of Radio

THE *Regent*   THE *Crown Prince*   THE *Duchess*   THE *Marquis*   THE *Baron*   THE *Baronet*   THE *Royal Highlander*

Air King Company 1947 advertisement from Radio News, December 1946.

General Electric 1941 model L-660 six-tube AC/DC radio with push-button tuning and interesting auto dashboard styling in heavy chrome and wooden cabinet.

Crosley 1938 model 587 six-volt DC and 110-volt AC five-tube upright wooden radio. Because the dial is marked in kilocycles and meters, it looks like a two-band radio but has only regular broadcast band. It has the beautiful, gold-mirrored Crosley "Fiver" dial.

go to the effort of finding the parts. Many parts are, of course, replaceable without too much trouble.

Broken coils and castings. Coils and castings hold parts in place and can give real difficulty if broken. Again, use judgment. If you can imagine how to fix a part, you probably can do it.

Fixable

Missing tubes. Be sure you know what tubes are missing. Numbers and letters identifying the tubes may be stamped on the tube sockets or next to them. There may be a paper in the cabinet showing the tube layout. Most tubes can be replaced, although they may be expensive. The older types usually cost more. If all the tubes are gone, you probably will spend more than you want to.

Rubber insulation flaking from wires. Wires can be replaced, as long as you know where they go and where they came from.

Grille cloth missing or torn. Torn cloth may be mended if it is not rotten. Replacement cloth can be installed easily.

Loudspeaker cone missing or torn. It may

be possible to repair if the damage is not too great. Speakers can be professionally reconed, also. Speaker replacement is not too difficult.

Knobs missing. If one knob is on hand, satisfactory replacements may be matched or molded. Several sources sell reproductions of knobs and pushbuttons. You may be able to substitute different but similar knobs.

Paint chipped or scratched on a plastic radio. You may be able to refinish the radio or get it refinished. Check with your favorite auto body shop. If you have a spray gun, you may be able to do it yourself.

Although this list will help you make an educated guess about the radio you are considering, there may be invisible problems that only careful examination and testing will reveal. You can tell much from a radio's appearance, however.

By the way, when buying at auction, don't put too much faith in the descriptions of the auctioneer, who may know very little about a set's condition.

Delco 1947 model R1231A brown Bakelite five-tube AC/DC radio from General Motors' electronics division.

Interstate Radio Company circa 1920s five-tube Neutradyne battery radio. The front panel is maroon with black swirls.

Philco 1942 model 42-PT95 five-tube AC/DC radio in wooden cabinet with plastic front. Knobs are 1948 Philco.

ANTIQUE RADIO RESTORATION GUIDE

RCA 1939 model 45X1 five-tube
AC/DC radio. This is a very small
brown Bakelite model.

Crosley 1951 model 11-100U five-
tube AC/DC Coloradio with
streamlined styling. This radio was
available in five different colors.

Philco 1955 model C-584 five-tube
AC/DC radio in maroon plastic
with light gray plastic grille.

Salt and pepper and cookie jar cop-
ies of an RCA table radio in tur-
quoise and black. All kinds of radio
collectibles are available.

Howard 1946 model 906 six-tube
AC wooden table radio with black
plastic front plate.

RCA 1963 model 3X521 five-tube
AC/DC radio. This is about as simple and homely as they come.

ANTIQUE RADIO RESTORATION GUIDE

Determining Price

When you have examined your prospective radio, make a guess of its overall condition. That guess, with a price guide or two, will help you set the price you're willing to pay. Here are some condition guidelines.

Excellent. This radio is in perfect working condition, but it may show a bit of wear. Knobs, dials, and case may show a little discoloring from age. This set is a rare find. It will be worth more than the price guide price.

Very good. This radio can readily be put in working condition although it might not actually work when bought. It may need a few easily replaced parts, like a tube, a few screws, or a power cord. There may be some minor cabinet wear or marking. Its appearance is good, and if the price is right, it is a good buy. It will price close to price guide price.

Good. Most of the sets you find will be in this condition. They are either functioning or easily repairable. The cabinets may need refinishing. There will be some missing or broken parts, but they can be restored. It will probably be worth half to two-thirds of the price guide value.

Fair. This radio does not work. It will take considerable effort, but it is repairable. It exhibits heavy wear and tear with many missing parts and, possibly, broken castings. Radios in this category present quite a challenge. They sell cheaply but are not for beginners. Don't pay too much for one of these—no more than one-third of the price guide value.

Poor. This set will be nearly impossible to repair since too many parts are missing, ruined, and/or damaged. The cabinet may show heavy damage as well. You've really got to want one of these sets to bother with it. Sometimes two sets of the same model in poor condition will provide enough parts to make one workable set, but generally speaking, these are junk. You may want one for parts if the price is low enough.

Remember this grading guide when it comes to pricing and buying a set. Most prices in guides will be for sets that are in very good condition. Excellent sets may command a sizable premium, whereas poor radios can be had for very little and are, sad to say, often worth very little.

2
How Does a Radio Work?

In order to do even basic radio repair, it is helpful to know some electronics theory. This chapter will provide that. If you wish to learn more, stop at your local library or bookstore and look over their books on basic electronics.

Electron Theory

Briefly, all matter in the universe is made of 106 fundamental materials called elements. Some are common—such as oxygen, hydrogen, carbon, and silicon. There are also rare and sometimes dangerous elements, such as radium. These elements in various combinations give us familiar things. For example, oxygen and hydrogen combine to make water.

An atom has a central body of positive charge consisting of protons and neutrons. This nucleus is surrounded by an equal negative charge of much smaller electrons. The variety of different elements are the result of differing numbers of protons and electrons.

When electrons are pulled free from their atoms, an electric current is produced. In some substances, called conductors, the electrons come loose quite easily. Since the charge of an electron is very small, many billions of them must be set in motion to produce a measurable current.

Electrons exist everywhere in nature, and loosely bound free electrons tend to be present in equal numbers in all places. But if a body has more electrons than do the bodies surrounding it, it is negatively charged. On the other hand, if a body lacks enough electrons to be neutral, it is positively charged.

If a positively charged body is brought into contact with a negatively charged body, electrons will flow from the negative to the positive until both bodies have the same number of free electrons and become neutral. Electrons are always attracted in the direction of a positive charge.

The charged bodies need not be brought into direct contact for the electrons to flow. A wire that acts as a conductor can connect them. Copper, because of its comparatively low price among good conductors, is used most frequently, but nearly all metals are fairly good conductors of electrons.

Resistance. Any conductor exerts a certain amount of opposition to the passage of electrons. This opposition is known as resistance. Silver, copper, and aluminum have little resistance. Iron has considerably more, and it may become hot when many electrons are retarded in their passage through it. A thick wire has less resistance than a thin wire of the same material because it has a greater cross-section, that is, more area in which the electrons can move.

Substances other than metals can have a very high resistance, permitting few electrons to pass through them. Most plastics, glass, rubber, and porcelain are good examples of common insulators.

The unit used to measure resistance is the ohm. Assume we have a battery that is producing an electron pressure of one volt. It is connected to push a current through a wire with one ohm of resistance. The electron flow, or current, through the wire will be one ampere (amp). Voltage, resistance, and the resultant current are interrelated in any circuit. In circuits where the direction of electron flow does not change often (DC), the relationship is expressed mathematically according to Ohm's Law: $I = E/R$. The symbol I stands for the current in amps, E for the voltage in volts, and R for the resistance in ohms.

Sources of electron flow. Two practical ways of producing substantial electron pressure or voltage exist: chemical generation and magnetic generation. Chemical generation is possible because certain substances in reaction to other substances produce either a shortage or an excess of electrons among them. The most common generators of this sort are batteries of the rechargeable, or single-service, type. The current produced by this device always moves in one direction, and its pressure, or voltage, depends on the substances of which it is made.

Magnetic generation is the principal sort used commercially. A wire in a moving magnetic field will have an electron pressure produced between its ends and can thus provide a current flow. This is the principle behind all generators. Generators can be designed to produce almost any voltage of either one-way (direct) current or alternating current.

Electric currents. These may flow in one direction only or change direction regularly. Single-direction flow is called direct current (DC), whereas a current that changes at regular intervals is called alternating current (AC). The change from one direction to another in AC does not happen instantaneously. Instead the flow will be wavelike, gradually increasing in intensity in one direction, then decreasing gradually to an absence of electron movement, followed by a reversal of current flow to a maximum and another decrease of current flow, and so on. The complete change from start to maximum and back is called one cycle, or hertz (Hz).

Fig. 2–1 will help you visualize this. The height of the curve shows voltage and rate of change through a complete positive and negative loop, or cycle. The frequency in U.S. power systems is generally 60 cycles per second at a voltage of about 115 volts. Audio frequencies vary from 20 to 20,000 cycles per second. Radio frequencies show rates of change from many thousands to many millions per second.

Magnetism. Another force important to ra-

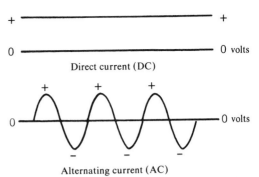
FIG. 2–1 *Alternating (AC) and direct (DC) electric currents.*

dios and electrical devices is magnetism. Transformers, motors and generators, loudspeakers, and other radio parts use magnetism. Like electricity, magnetism cannot be seen or felt, but its effects can be detected, measured, and used.

A magnet can attract iron or steel objects because it produces a force field. The magnet has two poles of opposite force, or polarity. If a magnet is brought close to a piece of iron, its force field produces an opposite field in the nearest end of the iron. The two oppositely magnetized poles attract.

In the same way, when two magnets are brought together, the oppositely magnetized poles will attract each other, whereas the similarly charged poles will repel each other. Fig. 2–2 shows how this force field is visualized. The lines do not actually exist, but they show the force and its direction.

An important property of the magnetic force field coming from a magnet's pole is that it decreases proportionately with the square of the distance from that pole. The strength of a field at two inches from a pole will be one-

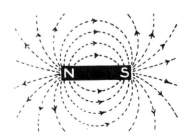
FIG. 2–2 *Magnetic field surrounding bar magnet.*

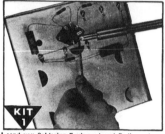

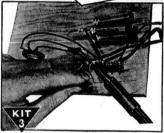
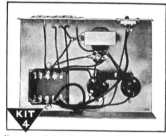

The National Radio Institute was one of the largest correspondence schools. These schools provided good basic instruction to students who applied themselves. This ad was seen in Radio News, September 1946.

fourth the strength at one inch. The field is strongest at the pole.

Magnetism can be produced by the flow of an electric current through a conductor. This is just the opposite of what happens in a generator, where the moving magnetic field produces an electric current. Every wire that carries a current has a magnetic field around it proportional to current strength and distance from the wire. By winding wire to form a coil, a much stronger magnetic field can be produced, since the field of each individual turn will add to the next and produce a stronger field, as can be seen in Fig. 2–3. That coil has a field much like the magnet in Fig. 2–2.

As we saw before, the magnetic field, or flux, is thought of as imaginary lines of force from one end of the coil or magnet to the other. Total magnetic flux depends on the number of turns of wire and on the strength of the current. If the current is high, fewer turns of thick wire will be required. If the current is weak, many turns of thin wire will be needed to produce the same magnetic force.

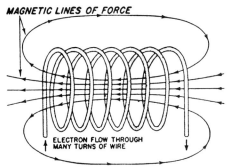

FIG. 2–3 *Coil with magnetic field.*

The magnetic flux of a coil can be increased greatly if a bar of iron is placed in the center of the coil, since the lines of force produced will be concentrated in the iron. A coil with an iron core will act exactly like a magnet as long as current flows through the coil.

Inductance and reactance. The ability of a coil to set up a magnetic field when current is flowing through it is called inductance. A coil with current flowing through it tends to oppose any increase or decrease of current flow. This opposition force in an inductance is called reactance and is proportional to the inductance of the coil. Inductance is measured in units called henries, and reactance is measured in ohms. The kind of reactance that inductances possess is called inductive reactance.

Reactance also depends on the rate of change of the current through the coil. A greater rate of change results in greater opposition or reactance in a coil with a certain inductance.

A useful result of reactance is that it allows direct (unchanging) current to flow through it easily while resisting (or choking) changing, or alternating, current. See Figs. 2–4 and 2–5 for examples of how air core and iron core transformers are put together.

If a coil with a magnetic field comes near another coil, an electrical pressure will be caused in the second coil, as long as the magnetic field is moving or changing. Energy will pass from one coil, called the primary coil, to the second, called the secondary coil, as long

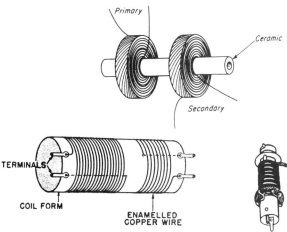

FIG. 2–4 *Radio frequency transformers* (R.F.T.).

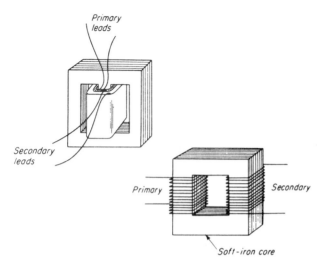

Primary leads

Secondary leads

Primary

Secondary

Soft-iron core

FIG. 2–5 *Iron-core transformer construction.*

as the field in the first coil is changing in intensity. The ratio of the voltage in the two coils is the ratio of the number of turns in those coils. If the secondary coil has more turns than the primary, it will have a higher voltage than the primary. If it has fewer turns, it will have a lower voltage.

Thus, this two-coil device can be used to transform one voltage into another, either higher or lower. For this reason it is called a transformer, one of the most useful devices in a radio set.

Capacitance. Two metal plates facing each other and separated by air or a thin layer of insulation called a dielectric make a condenser or capacitor. (The term capacitor came into more general use in the 1940s.) *Condenser* is the older term, but *capacitor* more accurately describes the action of the device. We will use the terms condenser and capacitor interchangeably.

If such a capacitor is connected to a battery, electrons will flow from the plate connected to the positive terminal of the battery, through the battery, to the opposite plate. If the battery is disconnected, the electrons will be stored on one plate. If the plates are reconnected by wire, the electrons will flow through the connecting wire to the other plate, thus equalizing the charge of electrons on each.

The capacitance, or storage ability, of a condenser depends on three things: the size of the plates, the space between the plates, and the dielectric (insulation) used. The larger the

plate area, the greater the capacity. The closer the plates, the greater that capacity as well. Fig. 2–6 illustrates how this works. Capacity also depends on the dielectric. For example, a capacitor of a certain physical size will have seven times the capacity with mica as an insulator as it would with air as the dielectric.

The unit of measurement of capacity is the farad. However, the farad is much too large a unit for radio work. A more useful unit is the microfarad (mfd.), which is $\frac{1}{1,000,000}$ of a farad. An even smaller unit is also found, the micromicrofarad (mmfd.), which is $\frac{1}{1,000,000}$ of a microfarad.

Capacitors or condensers not only store energy but are also important in radio work for another reason. If a condenser is connected in a circuit with direct current being supplied, the condenser will permit current to flow for a very short time while it is being charged. If alternating current is supplied, the capacitor will permit current to flow to some degree because the charging voltage is constantly changing. The faster the change, the easier the flow. This opposition to slow change or direct current is called reactance and is measured in ohms. This reactance is called capacitive reactance and is different from the reactance of coils, which is called inductive reactance. In fact, these two kinds of reactance tend to cancel each other, a fact useful for tuning circuits.

Condensers used to block DC while passing a wanted AC signal are called blocking or coupling condensers. Condensers wired to

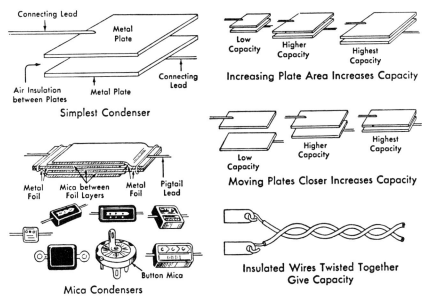

FIG. 2–6 *Mica condensers and condenser basics (from Markus).*

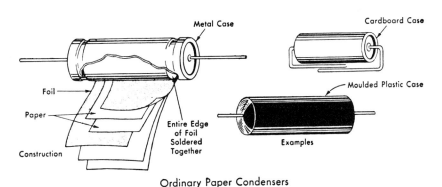

Ordinary Paper Condensers

FIG. 2–7 *Paper condenser construction.*

pass AC to ground while keeping DC in the circuit are called bypass condensers. A variable capacity condenser used to tune a resonant circuit is called a variable condenser or tuning condenser.

Smaller condensers used in old radios had waxed paper or mica as the dielectric. Fig. 2–7 shows the construction of several condensers. Variable and trimmer condensers generally use an air or mica dielectric. Fig. 2–8 gives drawings of these types.

Another important type of condenser, the electrolytic, has a very high capacity for its size. This is because its dielectric is chemically formed when the condenser is subject to a charging voltage. Fig. 2–9 shows how this type is put together. The dielectric is very thin and is capable of withstanding high voltages. The thinness of the dielectric gives the electrolytic its high capacity. These capacitors can be used as filters in power supplies and for low-frequency bypass tasks.

Ceramic condensers. Using a ceramic dielectric, these condensers are used in much the same places as paper condensers. They are very reliable.

Resonance. An especially useful result of the combination of inductance and capacity in a circuit is called resonance. Both the reactance of an inductance and the similar but

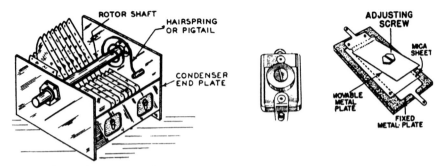

FIG. 2–8 *Variable and trimmer condensers.*

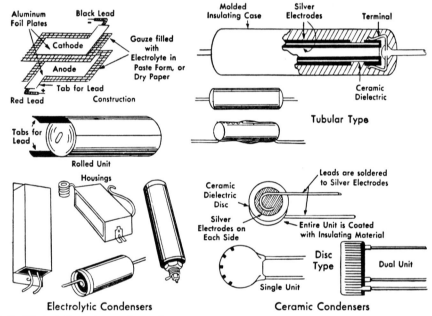

FIG. 2–9 *Electrolytic and ceramic condensers.*

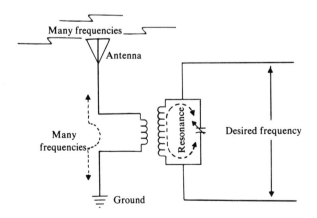

FIG. 2–10 *Frequency selection by tuned circuit.*

ANTIQUE RADIO RESTORATION GUIDE

opposite reactance of a condenser will change with a change in the frequency of the alternating current flowing in them. At a certain frequency, called resonance, these two reactances will be equal and cancel one another. Depending on the way the capacity and inductance are wired together, that resonant frequency either will be strengthened while all others are reduced, or it will be reduced more than all others. By varying either the capacity of the circuit or its inductance, this principle can be used to tune a circuit to a desired frequency. Fig. 2–10 shows how such a tuned circuit works. This is the method of choice for tuning receivers.

Radio Tubes

The device that made radio transmission and reception truly practical was the vacuum tube. Ordinarily a receiving tube consists simply of two or more electrodes inside a high vacuum glass or metal shell, see Fig. 2–11. The shell holds the vacuum necessary to maintain and control electron flow and keep filaments from burning up.

You recall that electrons are invisible charges of negative electricity capable of traveling thousands of miles per second. These flowing electrons make radio tubes possible.

A tube contains a number of parts. The cathode is the element that supplies electrons. A directly heated cathode consists of a special wire coated with a substance that, when heated, gives off electrons. The necessary heat is provided by passing an electric current through the filament wire. Examples of directly heated cathode or filament tubes are 45,

80, and '01A. Later, directly heated tube examples would be the 1U4 and 3S4.

An indirect or heater cathode tube has a heating element inside a metal sleeve from which it is electrically insulated. This sleeve is coated with a material that emits electrons. Most modern AC set tubes are of this kind. Typical tubes in older sets with this sort of cathode are 27 or 24A. Newer sets may use 12SA7, 50L6 or 35W4 types.

A diode tube has two working elements: a cathode to supply the electrons and a plate to attract and receive the flow. Fig. 2–12 shows a tube with two diodes within the same shell. Since electrons are negative in charge, they are attracted by a positively charged plate and flow to it. If the plate has a negative charge, on the other hand, no flow will take place. The diode acts as a one-way valve permitting electron flow in one direction only. Tube types 80, 6H6, and 35Z5 are examples of diodes. Diode tubes are used most frequently as rectifier tubes in power supplies or as detectors.

The triode is a three-element tube. The third element, called a control grid, is located between the cathode and plate and consists of a coiled wire with space between the loops (see Figs. 2–11 and 2–13).

The purpose of the grid is to control the flow of electrons to the plate. Since electrons are negative electrical charges, they are repelled and prevented from passing to the plate when a negative voltage is applied to the grid. When the grid becomes less negative it permits some

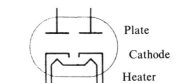
FIG. 2–12 *Dual section diode tube.*

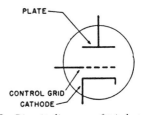
FIG. 2–13 *Circuit diagram of triode tube.*

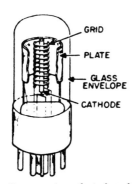
FIG. 2–11 *Construction of triode tube.*

General Electric 1946 model 220 brown Bakelite six-tube AC/DC two-band radio.

Motorola 1952 model 62X-13U green plastic six-tube AC/DC radio. Model 62X-11U featured walnut plastic; model 62X-12U had ivory plastic.

Zenith 1952 chassis 6J05 six-tube AC/DC radio in brown Bakelite with brass trim.

THE RCA TUBE TWINS SAY...

"WE'RE THE TUBES YOU CAN COUNT ON—

FOR FINER PERFORMANCE!"

THE best evidence of the *quality* that's built into every RCA radio tube is the fact that over 300 million of them have been bought by radio users.

For better radio reception, better tone, better volume — ask for RCA radio tubes. Built by the world's foremost radio organization, RCA radio tubes offer you the extra advantages of (1) the unmatched experience of RCA engineers in every phase of radio, (2) the unmatched research and manufacturing facilities of the only company making everything in radio.

No wonder RCA radio tubes are "the tubes of unquestioned quality"! No wonder they'll do a better job for you at low cost!

Ask your distributor, or send 10 cents to Camden, N. J., for a commemorative advertisement on RCA's television tube announcement.

RCA presents the "Magic Key" every Sunday, 2 to 3 p.m., E.S.T. on NBC Blue Network

RCA Radio Tubes

RCA Manufacturing Company, Inc., Camden, New Jersey
A Service of the Radio Corporation of America

RCA tube advertisement from Radio News, April 1938.

electrons to pass to the plate. A change of even a fraction of a volt on the grid is enough to either permit or stop the passage of electrons. The grid can easily vary the number of electrons moving through the tube. This ability of a small voltage change to affect a large current flow is called amplification. This important property makes it possible to increase very small signal voltages to usable levels. Any degree of amplification can be obtained simply by adding more stages (tubes) in a series. A tube also will work over a wide range of frequencies and can amplify radio frequencies as well as audio frequency signals.

In actual operation the grid usually is kept slightly negative to limit the flow of electrons. When you tune in a station, you are picking up a small electrical charge and adding it to the grid voltage on your tube, making it more or less negative and decreasing or increasing the electron flow. But the signal you pick up is not constant. It varies with the speech or music fed into the broadcaster's microphone, so the varying flow of electrons between the cathode and the plate can duplicate the program. After detection and sufficient amplification, there is a signal strong enough to run a loudspeaker.

A triode tube is problematic, however.

Some electrical capacity exists in the tube between the cathode and grid and the grid and plate. This acts as a small condenser wired between those parts and limits the possible amplification, or gain, of the tube. If too much amplification is demanded, enough of the signal will be fed back through the capacity of the tube to make the tube begin amplifying its own signal and oscillating at some unwanted frequency. However, this oscillation sometimes is wanted and controlled.

The invention of the tetrode tube solved this problem. The tetrode has four elements with two grids. The second grid, called a screen grid, is between the control grid and the plate (Fig. 2–14). It operates at a voltage similar to the plate but receives no varying signal current. Thus, it acts to shield the plate electronically from the grid. Instead of weakening the tube, this grid permits more amplification without oscillation.

Sometimes a third grid, called a suppressor grid, is added between the screen grid and the plate. This makes a pentode tube (Fig. 2–15). A pentode is capable of even higher amplification than a tetrode.

Tube types other than triode and dual diode will combine two or more working sets of elements in the same shell. Sometimes more grids are added and, used additionally, modify the same electron stream. An example of this

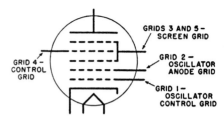

FIG. 2–16 *Pentagrid converter tube circuit.*

is the multigrid converter tube shown in Fig. 2–16. A careful examination of the electrical circuit often helps the repairer discover how a given tube works.

Circuit diagrams. Radio service information always includes a circuit diagram. This drawing shows the electrical paths within a radio, identifying wires with lines and parts with symbols. When examining the diagrams in this book you will need to know the symbols. Fig. 2–17 shows some of the common symbols used, particularly in older diagrams. Not all diagrams use identical symbols, but once you have used circuit diagrams a few times, you will be able to understand the differences.

Broadcasting and Receiving

In order to transmit a program, a radio broadcasting station must have several basic parts. Fig. 2–18 is, of course, a simplified diagram. Much more is involved in a working station, but always there must be five basic parts:

1. There must be some way to change sound pressure into an equivalent electrical signal. This is done by a microphone.
2. There must be a section designed to generate a radio frequency (R.F.) alternating current of the desired carrier frequency. This is done by the oscillator section.
3. There must be a section that will impress the audio frequency energy from the microphone onto the R.F. carrier. This is done by the modulator.
4. There must be some device that will cause the modulated energy to be radiated into space. This is done by the transmitting antenna.
5. There must be a source for the large amounts of energy required to transmit a

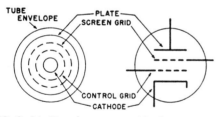

FIG. 2–14 *Tetrode or screen grid tube construction and diagram.*

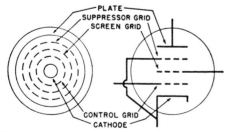

FIG. 2–15 *Pentode tube construction and circuit.*

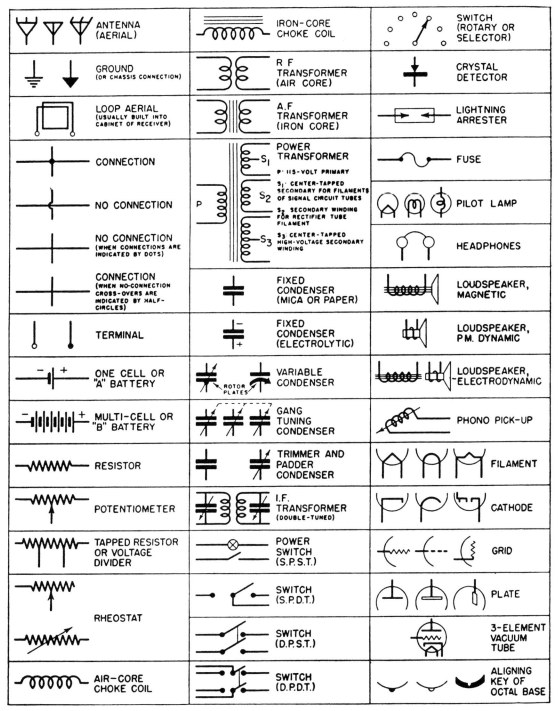

FIG. 2–17 *Schematic radio symbols.*

HOW DOES A RADIO WORK?

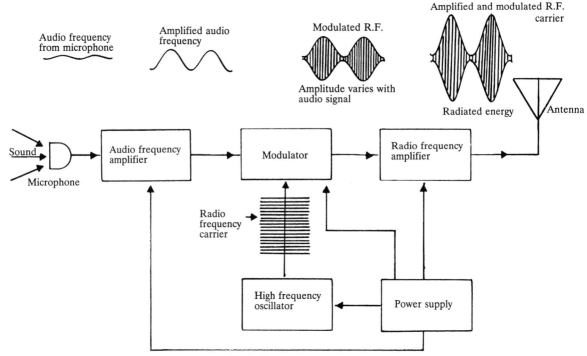

FIG. 2–18 *Basic transmitting station block diagram.*

strong signal. This is provided by the station's power supply.

A radio receiver must be provided with circuits that perform the opposite function of that performed by the transmitter. Figure Fig. 2–19 shows a basic receiver. Again, there are essential parts:

1. There must be some way of picking up the desired transmitted energy from space. This is done by the receiving antenna and the tunable circuits of the receiver.
2. There must be some way of recovering the audio frequency (A.F.) signal from the modulated radio frequency (R.F.) carrier. This is the task of the detector.
3. There must be some way of changing the A.F.'s electrical energy into sound. This is the function of the loudspeaker.
4. There usually must be a source of electrical energy for the receiver. This is the function of the power supply.

You'll be working with receivers rather than transmitters, and probably with the superhet-

erodyne. Fig. 2–20 gives an idea, in block form, of the parts that make a superheterodyne. The signal moves through the circuit from the top to the bottom of the diagram.

The antenna, a loop or piece of wire, picks up a wide variety of radio signals. The strength of these signals is only a few millionths of a volt, so they go to the R.F. amplifier to be strengthened. The R.F. amplifier is usually a tube that can be tuned by an inductance and capacitor from the tuning dial of the radio to provide maximum amplification of the station you want to hear.

This amplified signal goes next to the converter, where the modulated transmitter frequency is changed to a lower radio frequency, which can be amplified and tuned more efficiently.

This new lower frequency is called the intermediate frequency (I.F.). The I.F. passes through one or more amplifier stages, each consisting of a tube and tuned circuit set permanently to the I.F. frequency.

Now amplified even more, the I.F. goes to the detector, where the R.F. carrier frequency

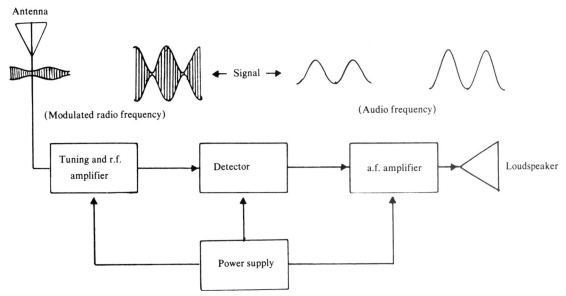

(Modulated radio frequency) ← Signal → (Audio frequency)

FIG. 2–19 *Basic radio receiver block diagram.*

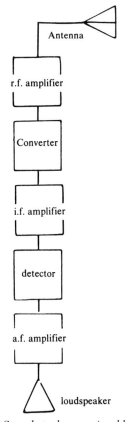

FIG. 2–20 *Superhetrodyne receiver block diagram.*

is removed and only the A.F. portion remains. This detector is frequently a diode-type rectifier.

Next, the A.F. amplifier increases the strength of this audio signal so that it can move the speaker voice coil and, finally, produce audible sound.

Simpler receiver designs were used in older sets. These are discussed, along with a more detailed explanation of the superheterodyne, in the chapter on receiver theory. The workings of individual circuits are explained at some length in Chapter 8.

3
Cleaning the Radio

Resist the temptation to plug in your radio right away. Do not apply power until after you have done some preliminary checking. A good cleaning at this point will make later work easier. Remember, work in a well-lit place and be gentle. Clean your radio but don't scrub it. Don't move parts or wires any more than is necessary. You do not want to add to the problems your radio might have.

You will need to remove the chassis, the metal base on which the radio itself is built. Unless the panel on which the controls are mounted is part of the chassis so that the whole thing slides out in one piece, you will need to remove the knobs. Many knobs have a small screw on the side. Use a small screwdriver to loosen the screw and remove the knob. Unless all the knobs are identical, make a diagram and number them so you can replace them in their former positions. If a knob has no screw, it is designed to pull off. Be careful, because it may stick. If you pry off a knob with a screwdriver, protect the panel and do not break the knob. Plastic knobs may be brittle.

The chassis may simply lift from its cabinet. More often it will be bolted through the bottom. If you turn over the set to loosen these screws, be careful to support the chassis and protect it from a fall. Before actually removing the chassis, check to see where the loudspeaker is attached. If it is connected directly to the chassis, as it is in many small radios, leave it in place and remove the complete unit. If the loudspeaker is fastened to the front of the cabinet, unplug the wires that attach it. In some radios it will be bolted to the cabinet and still

be permanently wired into the chassis. If this is the case, loosen the chassis, slide it out as far as possible, and unfasten the speaker. Be careful; this is a clumsy arrangement. Protect the front of the speaker cone from damage.

Any speaker can be damaged rather easily when it is out of the cabinet. A good way of protecting it is to cut a circle of cardboard the right size to cover the speaker and tape it over the speaker. Later, when testing the receiver, you may want to uncover the speaker for better sound. Any speakers you are storing for later use should be protected this way.

Now we return to the cabinet. Any wires still attached to the cabinet may be antenna wires. Unfasten them from the chassis, labeling the place of their attachment. If the wires lead to switches on the cabinet, the switches must be removed with the chassis.

Once it is free, clean the chassis, beginning on top, using a vacuum cleaner and soft paintbrush. Carefully and gently dust all reachable crevices and cracks with the paintbrush and remove debris using the vacuum. Here a small compressor is helpful for blowing out the dust under parts. Hold the compressor hose in one hand and the vacuum in the other, and suck up the dust as it is blown free. Now remove one tube at a time to avoid confusion and to dust its socket. Remove and replace each tube several times to clean socket contacts. Clean tubes with a damp cloth, taking care not to rub off identification numbers.

Turn over the chassis. If the bottom is clean, leave it alone. Even if it is dirty, do not vacuum it directly. Use the soft brush and

Monitor 1946 model TA 56M Bakelite case five-tube AC/DC radio. This is neither a known brand nor a very interesting radio.

Motorola 1952 model 72XM22 seven-tube AC/DC design FM/AM radio in green-painted plastic (and also available in gray). Interesting styling, but the condition of this example is poor.

Silvertone 1941 model 7054 five-tube AC/DC brown wooden table radio. It features push buttons and European styling.

IGA wooden table radio. There is no identification of manufacturer on this radio, but the IGA food chain logo appears on the front panel. This radio may have been sold in grocery stores.

Guild "American Spice Chest" walnut-colored spice chest transistor radio with two drawers and multicolored carriage print on the speaker grille. (Another model lacks the carriage print.)

Aiwa 1967 model AR-111 transistor portable AM/FM radio. This is a large and heavy example of a better early imported Japanese radio.

compressor again to remove accessible dirt. Vacuum up debris, but keep the cleaner away from parts and wires. Insulation on wires may be very brittle and could flake off. Avoid the temptation to turn screws, unless a mounting screw is obviously loose. You can dust them off or blow any loose dust from around them.

If you find any mouse nesting material on top or inside the chassis, remove everything you can with tweezers. Be careful not to break any fine wires around or on the coils. Shake the chassis over a wastebasket to get seed hulls and other bits to fall out, and proceed with your normal cleaning.

You may find some oily, waxy spots on the chassis from parts that have become too hot. Don't try to clean them up now; later you can use naphtha (lighter fluid) and a rag to clean them. First, let's get the radio working.

Clean the cabinet with thorough use of the vacuum brush, using the crevice tool and paintbrush to get into corners. Dust thoroughly to remove as much loose matter as possible, then clean the cabinet, inside and out, top and bottom, with a cloth dampened in turpentine. Dry all surfaces. If veneer is coming loose, use care. Be careful around the cloth covering the speaker opening, as it is old and will tear easily. A light dusting will suffice.

Before you set the cabinet aside, remove the loudspeaker, if you haven't already done so. It will be needed for later testing with the chassis. Again, the speaker may simply lift from the cabinet, or it may be bolted or screwed to the cabinet panel. Clean the speaker as carefully as you did the chassis. Use caution, as the paper cone on the speaker probably will be brittle and easily damaged. Protect it as mentioned above.

Now store the clean cabinet until the radio is repaired and working. Your next step is a careful examination of the chassis.

If the chassis smells badly of mouse urine, it may not be saveable. As a last resort try a thorough washing of the chassis, but don't do this if your radio has a power transformer, as it probably will be ruined. If there is a loudspeaker attached to the chassis it will need to be removed since it is sure to be ruined. Remove all tubes as well, noting which sockets they went into.

Wash the chassis thoroughly in water. A kitchen sink sprayer is a help. You can use a small amount of dishwashing detergent in some water, but clean water does well. Wash and rinse, wash and rinse, until the smell is gone. You will be amazed at the amount of dirt you'll get out of that chassis.

When you are done, make sure the water drains out of everything. Hold the chassis in various ways and shake it. Again, if you have a compressor, blow water out wherever you can.

Now set the chassis aside for several weeks in a warm and dry place so it dries thoroughly. You may have damaged some parts that will need to be replaced, but you also may have rescued the radio. Don't wash unless there is nothing else you can do. Once the chassis is bone dry, you can proceed with testing.

4
Examining the Radio

As you cleaned your radio, you probably took the first steps in examining it. A more thorough, separate examination is important and will spare you later grief. Many of your set's problems or faults will be visible if you look at it carefully in good light.

As you examine your set, remember that there will be an orderly flow of electrical energy through it. There is nothing mysterious about it. Take the time to write down everything. If you remove a wire, note where it came from. Use bits of colored tape to code wires and their connections. Keep notes and draw pictures of anything you change. Don't trust your memory! If you find yourself getting frustrated or tired, quit for a time. That radio has been waiting many years for you to come along, and it can wait a few more days.

Fig. 4–1 shows top and bottom views of a typical "midget" superheterodyne radio manufactured in the mid-1930s. In Chapter 11 you will find the same views of a 1950s five-tube superheterodyne. As you examine the parts of your set, compare them with the drawings and try to identify each part.

If anything seems to be wrong with a part, consult Chapter 8 on repair in this book. Here are some readily visible parts that can tip you off to trouble.

Tubes. Order missing tubes immediately. You can't do anything without them. Make sure they are in the right sockets. If you have access to a tube tester, check the tubes that remain, but remember that a tube may test satisfactorily and still not work in a particular radio.

Tuning condensers. Fig. 4–2 illustrates a variable condenser and small mica trimmer condensers. Try to turn the tuning knob on your set. If it does not move, don't force it. Use television tuner-cleaner spray on the points where shafts should move. Follow with a little WD-40 once the system is freed. Check for bent plates on the condenser, and straighten them carefully if they are binding. Clean any remaining dust from between the plates. By placing a light where it will shine through the plates, you can see if any junk is trapped, and if so, use a compressor to blow it out. A clean piece of thick paper can be cut and pushed gently between the plates to clean them out.

If the dial cord is broken, discover how it connected the tuning shaft and condenser. If you can't, you will have to obtain service instructions for your set. See Chapter 8 for some typical dial arrangements which may help you understand yours. If it needs replacing, use proper dial cord, if possible. (Sometimes heavy nylon thread will substitute.) If the dial cord slips where it loops around the tuning shaft, rub the cord at that point with a small amount of powdered rosin.

When work on the tuning condenser is completed, turn the movable plates so that they are inside the fixed plates to prevent accidental damage. By the way, if you have to wait to get dial cord or a service diagram, you can still test the set by turning the condenser by hand.

Electrolytic condensers. Fig. 4–3 shows some typical styles, but electrolytic condensers come in all shapes and sizes. They filter

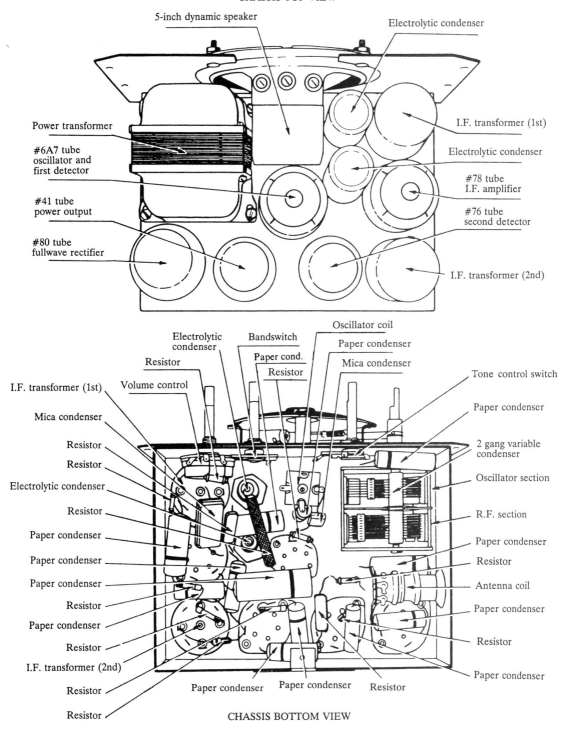

CHASSIS TOP VIEW

5-inch dynamic speaker

Electrolytic condenser

Power transformer

#6A7 tube
oscillator and
first detector

#41 tube
power output

#80 tube
fullwave rectifier

I.F. transformer (1st)

Electrolytic condenser

#78 tube
I.F. amplifier

#76 tube
second detector

I.F. transformer (2nd)

Oscillator coil

Electrolytic
condenser

Bandswitch

Paper condenser

Mica condenser

Paper cond.

Resistor

Resistor

Volume control

I.F. transformer (1st)

Mica condenser

Resistor

Resistor

Electrolytic condenser

Resistor

Paper condenser

Paper condenser

Paper condenser

Resistor

Paper condenser

Resistor

I.F. transformer (2nd)

Resistor

Resistor

Paper condenser

Paper condenser

Resistor

Tone control switch

Paper condenser

2 gang variable
condenser

Oscillator section

R.F. section

Paper condenser

Resistor

Antenna coil

Paper condenser

Resistor

Paper condenser

CHASSIS BOTTOM VIEW

FIG. 4–1 *Top and bottom view of superheterodyne receiver.*

33

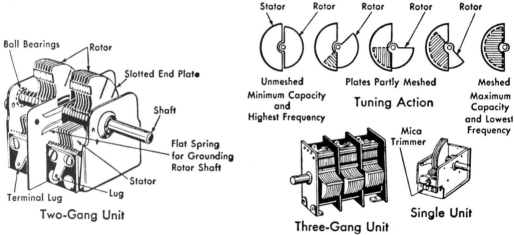

FIG. 4–2 *Tuning condenser information (from Markus).*

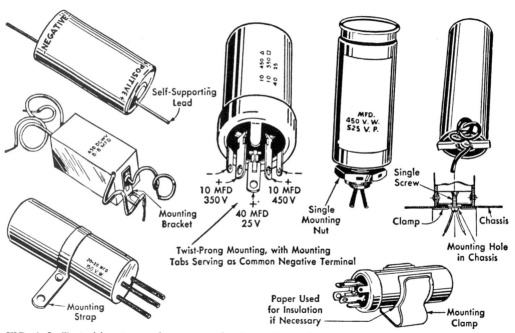

FIG. 4–3 *Typical housings and mountings for electrolytic condensers (from Markus).*

(smooth out) the direct current used by the tubes in your set. They are usually marked with rather high capacities, in the range of 4 to 50 mfd., as opposed to similar-looking paper condensers, which are usually .5 mfd. capacity or less. Corroded or swollen electrolytic condensers are worthless. Replace them with units of equal or greater capacity and equal or greater working voltage. Newer filter con-

densers are much smaller than the original parts. It's a good idea to replace suspicious-looking filters before trying out your set.

Paper condensers. Fig. 4–4 shows some typical styles. They may be in square metal cans or in plastic tubes or rectangles, but most often they are in cardboard tubes sealed with wax. It is hard to tell if they are bad by simply looking. If a wax-filled one has lost all wax out

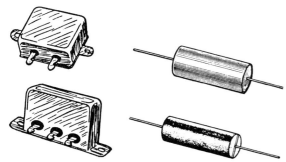

FIG. 4–4 *Typical bathtub condensers (left) and paper condensers (right).*

of the ends, it probably has shorted and should be replaced. Paper condensers used in bypass situations, where there is high voltage on one side, are prone to failure. The capacity and working voltage usually will be printed on the condenser. Sometimes they will have color bands to identify the capacity. See Fig. 4–5 for the color code, which resembles the resistor color code. Replace with the same capacity, plus or minus 25 percent, and the same or greater working voltage. Modern condensers, or capacitors, are much smaller and better. Often they are small enough to be put inside the case of the old part, if you want to be strictly authentic.

Mica and ceramic condensers. These small plastic rectangles, discs, or tubes are very reliable because of their good dielectric. They sometimes open but seldom short-circuit. Fig.

4–6 shows some of the variety of circuit diagram symbols used for condensers.

Volume controls and rheostats. Fig. 4–7 illustrates some examples of these resistors. These variable resistors have their own problems. Wire-wound units break, and carbon controls become dirty and noisy. This causes a scratching sound when the radio is on and the control is turned. To rectify this, spray a good television tuner-cleaner into the control. In fact, spraying all controls in this manner is a good idea. Wipe up any cleaner that runs out of the control, as it will just collect dust. Faulty volume controls aren't detectable by eye. Tone controls behave in the same way and have the same problems.

Resistors. Figs. 4–8, 4–9, and 4–10 give examples of two basic types of resistors and the color code used to mark the resistance of carbon resistors.

Wire-wound resistors usually carry quite a bit of power. Problems with them often are caused by a broken wire in the resistance element. Units with the resistance wires in the open are likely to corrode, but units sealed in ceramic are reliable.

Carbon resistors are smaller and nearly always color coded. About their only fault is that they burn, which requires replacement. They sometimes will change resistance after years of use. Suspect them if later testing indicates that there is a problem in that stage of the radio. Also, there probably will be a fault in the tube or condenser that drew too much current through the resistor and caused the burning or

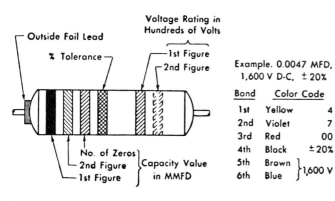

Example. 0.0047 MFD, 1,600 V D-C, ± 20%

Band	Color Code	
1st	Yellow	4
2nd	Violet	7
3rd	Red	00
4th	Black	± 20%
5th	Brown	}1,600 V
6th	Blue	

Color	Significant Figure	No. of Zeros	Capacity Tolerance
Black	0		± 20%
Brown	1	0	
Red	2	00	
Orange	3	000	± 30%
Yellow	4	0000	± 40%
Green	5	00000	± 5%
Blue	6	000000	
Violet	7		
Gray	8		
White	9		± 10%

FIG. 4–5 *Condenser color codes (from Markus).*

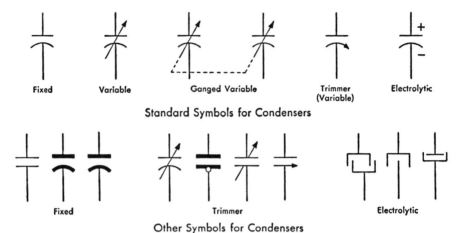

Fixed Variable Ganged Variable Trimmer (Variable) Electrolytic

Standard Symbols for Condensers

Fixed Trimmer Electrolytic

Other Symbols for Condensers

FIG. 4–6 *Circuit diagram symbols for condensers (from Markus).*

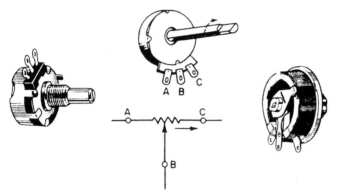

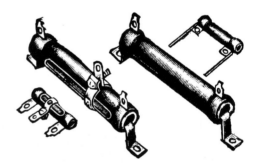

FIG. 4–7 *Volume controls, power rheostat and circuit diagram for volume control.*

change. Unfortunately, when a resistor burns, so does its color code, and a circuit diagram is necessary to find it out. With experience, however, you often can make an educated guess.

Transformers and chokes. Fig. 4–11 shows examples of iron core low-frequency transformers. These are easy to identify since they have iron cores, are bulky, and usually are painted black. They may be used to provide correct voltages for the set or to connect stages. Unless they have burned badly and are charred, it is difficult to tell by looking at them if they are all right. They may leak a little wax or tar with age, but this does not always indicate trouble.

Radio frequency transformers and coils. Fig. 4–13 shows some of the wide variety of these. They come in all shapes and sizes. Some are shielded inside aluminum cans; some are open and, usually, covered with a

FIG. 4–8 *Various power resistors.*

thick coat of wax. Most frequently, they connect antennas to the radio and interconnect radio frequency stages. If they are burned, they must be replaced. Faults beyond that are difficult to see. Note: if there are any screw adjustments with the coil or transformer, do *not* adjust. Some of these adjustments are critical, and since they were originally correct, proba-

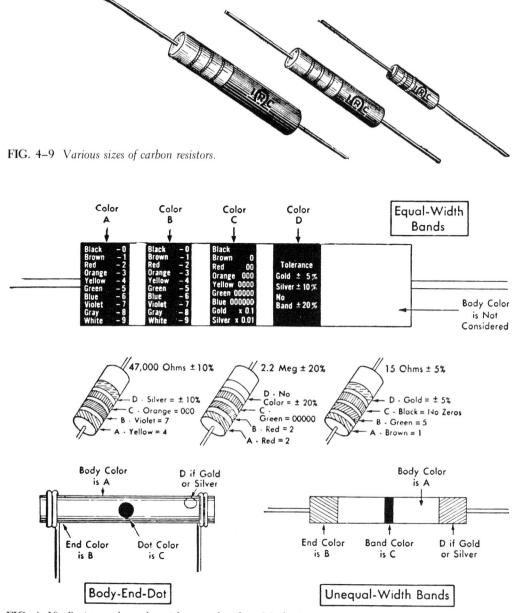

FIG. 4–9 *Various sizes of carbon resistors.*

FIG. 4–10 *Resistor color codes with examples (from Markus).*

bly they are still close. Wait until the set is working before touching them.

A very common R.F. transformer is the I.F. transformer used in all superheterodyne receivers. Sometimes the primary and secondary windings of the transformer are tuned by small built-in variable condensers, and at other times by moving in and out a powdered iron core. Both types are shown in Fig. 4–14.

In circuit diagrams I.F. transformers have several designations. Fig. 4–15 shows some of the more common.

Loudspeakers. Examples are shown in Fig. 4–16. Sets made in the 1920s converted the

EXAMINING THE RADIO

RCA 1933 model R28P chassis two-band five-tube AC "midget" radio, partially restored.

Philco circa late 1920s model 271 magnetic loudspeaker in brown-painted metal.

audio tube's electrical signal into sound in many strange ways, but by the 1930s the dynamic speaker was almost universal. Two types of dynamic speakers are common. One type produces the necessary strong magnetic field for the voice coil to act on by means of a large coil of wire, called the field coil. This obtains power from the radio's high-voltage power supply. Sometimes it was used as a filter choke in that supply.

Later, strong permanent magnets were developed, and these replaced the field coil as a source for the magnetizing field.

After you have dusted carefully the surface to be fixed, small rips in the brittle cone can be repaired with household glue or magic mend-

FIG. 4-11 *Typical iron-core transformers.*

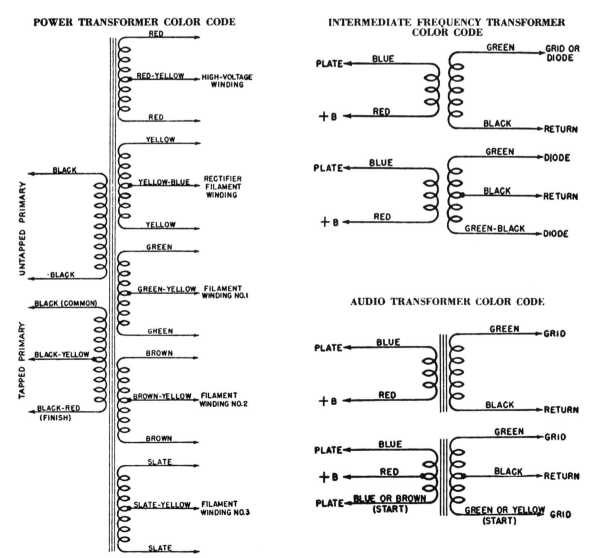

POWER TRANSFORMER COLOR CODE

RED

RED-YELLOW — HIGH-VOLTAGE WINDING

RED

YELLOW

YELLOW-BLUE — RECTIFIER FILAMENT WINDING

YELLOW

GREEN

GREEN-YELLOW — FILAMENT WINDING NO.1

GREEN

BROWN

BROWN-YELLOW — FILAMENT WINDING NO.2

BROWN

SLATE

SLATE-YELLOW — FILAMENT WINDING NO.3

SLATE

BLACK

·BLACK

UNTAPPED PRIMARY

BLACK (COMMON)

BLACK-YELLOW

BLACK-RED (FINISH)

TAPPED PRIMARY

INTERMEDIATE FREQUENCY TRANSFORMER COLOR CODE

PLATE ← BLUE   GREEN → GRID OR DIODE

+B ← RED   BLACK → RETURN

PLATE ← BLUE   GREEN → DIODE

                      BLACK → RETURN

+B ← RED   GREEN-BLACK → DIODE

AUDIO TRANSFORMER COLOR CODE

PLATE ← BLUE   GREEN → GRID

+B ← RED   BLACK → RETURN

PLATE ← BLUE   GREEN → GRID

+B ← RED   BLACK → RETURN

PLATE ← BLUE OR BROWN (START)   GREEN OR YELLOW (START) → GRID

FIG. 4-12° *Power transformer, I.F. transformer, and audio transformer color codes.*

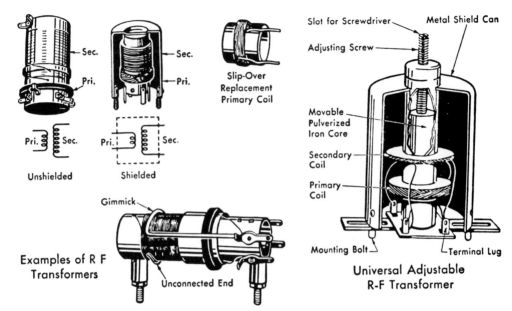

FIG. 4–13 *Typical R.F. coils found in receivers (from Markus).*

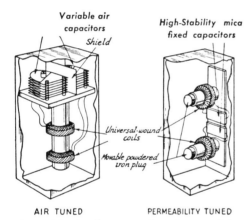

FIG. 4–14 *Condenser-tuned and permeability-tuned I.F. transformers (illustration courtesy of American Radio Relay League).*

ing tape. Check to see if the cone is warped by placing your hands at nine and three o'clock while facing the front of the speaker. Place your thumbs near the center of the speaker and gently push in the cone. It should spring out again without any rubbing noise if it is not warped. If it is warped, see Chapter 8 on repair. Electrical faults in the speaker will be invisible.

Switches. These will be either enclosed power switches or open-contact tone, band, or phono switches. Fig. 4–17 shows some ways switches are shown in circuits. Sometimes a sticking power switch can be freed if you spray some television tuner-cleaner into it and switch it off and on several times with the power unplugged. Open switches are often corroded. Spray contacts with television tuner-cleaner and operate the switch. Cut narrow strips of bond paper, push them between the closed contacts, and slide the paper in and out to polish the contacts.

Wire. Check the power line and plug. If it is rubber and rotted, replace it now with a similar style of wire. If the plug is removable, attach it to the new wire. Examine the chassis wires. If they are cloth insulated, they will give you no problems. If they have a rubber covering, it will have hardened. If some insulation has flaked off and the wire is touching any metal, the wire will have to be either replaced or taped. Once you start repair work, the hardened insulation will fall off rapidly. As long as the insulation is in place—even if it is hard—it will do its job.

Use your judgment throughout your examination. Replace only parts that are obviously bad, and write down anything you think might cause problems later. Finally, remember that great motto of the radio service profession: *If it ain't broke, don't fix it.*

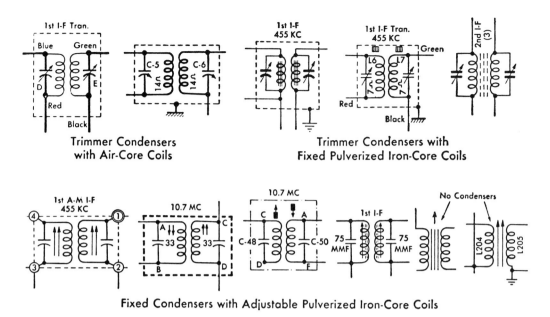

Trimmer Condensers
with Air-Core Coils

Trimmer Condensers with
Fixed Pulverized Iron-Core Coils

Fixed Condensers with Adjustable Pulverized Iron-Core Coils

FIG. 4–15 *Circuit diagrams for different I.F. transformers (from Markus).*

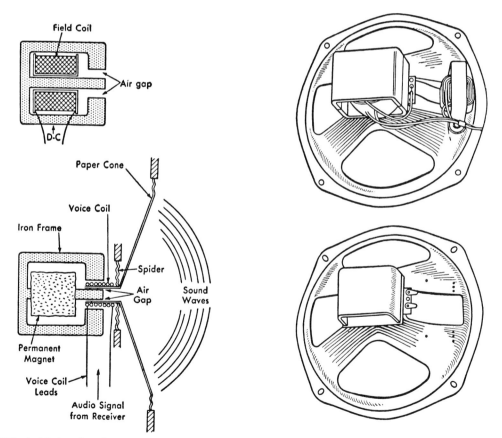

FIG. 4–16 *Loudspeaker construction and examples. Top has output transformer mounted on speaker (from Markus).*

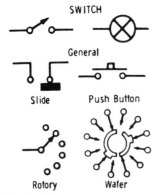

FIG. 4–17 *Switch circuit diagrams.*

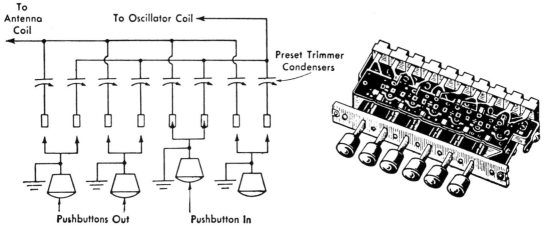

FIG. 4–18 *Circuit and example of pushbutton tuning switch (from Markus).*

5
Safety Precautions

A restorer should take certain safety precautions to work safely. Anyone working with electronics needs to be careful first with electricity, then with fire, then with burns, and finally with cuts and abrasions. The most serious concern is with electricity.

Electricity

Working with old electronic components involves working with electricity. Electricity is a wonderful friend and a hard-working servant, but it can kill.

You need to know what you are doing and be careful when working with electricity at any voltage higher than a few volts. Low voltages at high currents can cause burns; higher voltages, even at low currents, can cause nerve damage, interrupted breathing, and heart stoppage. This happens because the electric current flowing in the body damages the body's nerve communication system, which depends on small, carefully controlled electric currents in the nervous system. Cardio-pulmonary resuscitation (CPR) and immediate medical help must be provided to treat serious shock.

Think of the simple circuit shown in Fig. 5–1. A voltage (V) is applied to a resistance (R), and in flowing through that resistance produces heat. That is fine if the resistance is your electric toaster or the filament in a radio tube, but not if that resistance is your body.

This can happen in several ways. Let us say that the voltage is the 120 volts you find at your electrical outlet. If you have damp shoes and hands, and your hand touches point A while your shoes are on a damp floor at B, a dangerously high current may flow through you— through your heart and lungs and out point B. Your body's electrical resistance will be only a few hundred ohms, and the current will be deadly. If hands and shoes are dry, your resistance will be many thousands of ohms, making the shock much less dangerous.

But how does one side of the electrical line get connected to ground at B? The return of any household electrical system is always connected to normal earth ground, so if any part of your body touches that ground, and you touch the hot side at A, you will be a resistor.

There are several ways to cope with this problem in relation to 120-volt household current. We can first insulate the resistor (that's you) at points A or B, so that no current can flow through you to ground. Second, we can measure the current carefully coming in at

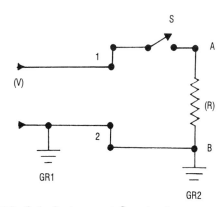

FIG. 5–1 *Basic current flow circuit.*

Weston circa early 1930s model 45 laboratory type DC voltmeter.

Two isolation transformers (left) and an adjustable voltage autotransformer (right). These are useful electronics shop accessories.

point 1 and going out at point 2 on the diagram. If the amount of current coming in at 1 is not exactly equal to the amount leaving at 2, we know some is getting to ground some way other than through the electric lines. Knowing this, we can build a device that will shut off the current at switch S before very much can flow. This is exactly what a ground fault interrupter (GFI) does. It examines the current coming in at 1 and out at 2 to the electrical system return (GR1). If you are resistance A, and current starts flowing through you to GR2 ground, which is connected by wire to the line return GR1, the GFI will detect it and shut off the power at switch S. You might notice a little tingle, that's all.

My shop is in a basement that is often damp. I run my whole shop through a GFI. Since any ordinary outlet can be replaced with a GFI, it is not hard to protect yourself from the line current. Remember, a GFI will work only on a three-wire system with a separate ground wire.

Another piece of equipment I always use when working on any radio is an isolation transformer. An isolation transformer has primary and secondary windings of equal length, so it puts out the same voltage that goes into it. In Fig. 5–2 you can see an isolation transformer placed in the circuit before the resistance.

Now there is no direct electrical connection between the A side of resistance (R) and the 120-volt electrical system. Any thing—or person—touching point A to GR1, the power line return, will not have current flowing through it since A is not connected to the power line. Only if the person connects A and B as in Fig. 5–2 will current flow through him. The transformer will protect a person from the 120-volt line, whether that line is protected by a GFI or not. See Chapter 12 for more information on isolation transformers.

While I always use an isolation transformer on any piece of equipment I am repairing, its use is essential on AC/DC sets, which may have one side of the power line attached to the chassis.

Even if an isolation transformer is used and you have a GFI protecting your shop, you can still receive a serious shock. In Fig. 5–3, if you contact A with one hand and B with the other, you will still become the resistor (R) and may have a dangerous current flow through you.

Never poke your finger in a chassis that is turned on or even plugged in. Always poke, prod, or tap with an insulated stick or rod. *Never* steady the chassis with one hand while working in it with the other. Again, you might easily become the resistor (R). Remember, there can be voltages in excess of 400 volts on the underside of a chassis. If in doubt, check with a voltmeter to see where these voltages are before doing anything under the chassis. *Never*

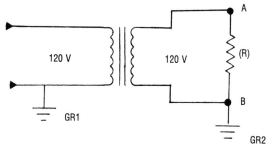

FIG. 5–2 *Isolation transformer protection.*

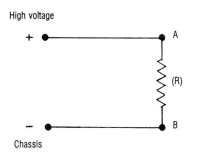

FIG. 5–3 *Never become a resistor*—you may receive a serious shock.

change parts without turning off the receiver and pulling the power plug. It is also a good idea to short-circuit one of the electrolytic filter capacitors to the chassis after you have turned off the receiver and before you do any work. Sometimes there can be an electrical charge on the capacitor that has not leaked off. It won't hurt you, but it can give you a real surprise.

Fire

The fire hazard with old electronic equipment is not great if a person uses common sense. Never leave old equipment on at full-line voltage unsupervised. Only after you know that it is in good working order can you leave it unattended. If you have cleaned the chassis carefully and have brought it slowly up to full voltage, you probably will not have troubles.

Parts that may burn or cause fire usually involve the power sections of the radio. Tubes, particularly rectifier and power output tubes, can be very hot while operating. Do not let them rest on paper or any flammable material. Metal power tubes can be very hot. Resistors,

particularly power resistors or ballast resistors, which look like tubes, can be a fire hazard even at their normal operating temperatures. Transformers can become very warm to the touch after they have been operating for an hour or more. They are not a fire hazard at their normal temperatures.

If a power supply is faulty, a resistor may burn, making a small fire. A power transformer, if it starts to burn, produces a large amount of very acrid smoke. *If anything in a receiver you are testing starts to smoke, pull the plug.* The burning likely will stop as soon as the power is removed, although some smoke may persist.

If you have a serious chassis fire, first remove power from the chassis. Next, ventilate the room if possible and leave it once you are certain that the fire has stopped. With the power removed, the smoke will subside in a couple of minutes. If the fire has spread outside of the chassis, call for help. I keep a dry (B-C) chemical extinguisher in my shop, but I have never had to use it. Fires in radios are generally localized in a small area. Watch out for them, but they are not generally dangerous. However, do not breathe the fumes from burning parts for an extended period.

Burns

There are two ways you are likely to receive burns when working with old radios. First, you can get localized burns from parts of the radio. Tubes are the first cause—rectifier and power tubes can be very hot, and metal ones very hot indeed. Power resistors can give some nasty small burns, even at normal operating temperatures.

The other way you get burns is from soldering irons or solder splashes. The burns are small but painful. My standard treatment for any small burn is to run cold water over the affected part until it no longer hurts. Then I go back to work, and anytime the burn starts hurting again, I return to the cold water. I will cover it only if it blisters or if the skin is broken. The kinds of burns you get in this work are small and annoying but usually not dangerous. If you should feel faint or have any other strange reactions, however, seek a doctor's advice immediately.

General 1938–1939 unknown model AM radio in ivory-painted plastic with red numbers on the dial and ivory push buttons. Probably made by Belmont of Chicago.

General Electric 1960 model T155B cocoa plastic six-tube AC/DC AM radio.

General, circa late 1950s, blue plastic five-tube AM/FM radio of Japanese manufacture. Although the front markings are in English, all of the back and chassis markings are Japanese and it does not have the US FM band. The only number resembling a model number is R85 737.

Cuts and Abrasions

The kinds of cuts you will get are of the usual sort, from small knives or pliers that slip. If there is no serious bleeding and no sign of traumatic shock, clean and protect the wound and go on from there. Always make sure you have examined and protected any wound. Make sure you do not have any dirt or foreign matter in the wound before you cover it.

Eye Protection

It is best to have some eye protection when working. Fumes can be irritating and solder splashes dangerous. A shop is not a high-risk area for eye damage, but good sense should prevail. Do not get your face close to your work if you are soldering, as hot solder flux may spatter if something slips or comes loose. Eyeglasses give enough protection for routine work. If you wear contact lenses or don't wear glasses, you might want a good pair of shop glasses. Always wear safety glasses when using power tools around your shop.

If anything should enter an eye, or if your eyes should become irritated by fumes, wash the eyes generously with cool water and quit work for a while. Seek help if something seems to be trapped in the eye or if it stays irritated for some time. You must be the judge, but remember how important your eyes are. Err on the side of caution.

Fumes and Smoke

The long-term breathing of any fumes can have negative health effects. Except for smoke filling a room, however, the exposure experienced by a part-time radio repairer is limited. It is still a good idea to avoid the fumes from chemicals or solder as much as possible. If you develop headaches from using any chemical, discontinue its use and let your shop clear of fumes before you go back. Work in a ventilated place and, if fumes are noticeable to you, use a small fan to clear your work area.

6
Trying Out Your Radio

Once you have given your radio a careful examination and repaired obvious problems like bad power cords or disconnected wires, you are ready to try out your set.

Remember the basic rules of Chapter 4 on examining your radio: use your eyes, use your head, write everything down, and don't work too long. These apply to all the tasks you will perform.

The first time you turn on a radio is always a bit frightening. Now you find out the true operating condition of your set. Remember, there was probably one thing that went wrong with the set, putting it out of action and into the attic. During the years your radio has been in storage, other parts may have deteriorated also. Don't expect perfect results the first time you try. Your goal is to find the one thing that stopped your set in the first place.

You now want to receive a station through the set, however faintly. After that, you can tune it up and work on improving reception.

Once you have the correct voltages, the easiest sets to test are the battery sets. Make sure the set is turned off and that all rheostats are turned fully counterclockwise. Hook up the power, making sure you have the right polarity. That means the positive (+) sides of batteries or power supplies go to positive terminals, and negative (−) sides to negative terminals. See to it that you have the correct voltages as well. If your voltages are correct, you probably will not hurt anything when you power up. Turn on your set, turn up the rheostats about halfway, and go to the What to Listen to and Look For section in this chapter.

When you fire up an AC set, you must be careful, or you may literally fire it up. Applying full-line voltage immediately may damage the set's power supply. It's far better to bring an AC set's power supply to full voltage slowly, using a variable voltage isolation transformer. These units are costly, but they allow you to increase the line voltage on a radio a few volts at a time. The isolation transformer also may have its own fuse in case the radio has none. The voltage on the set is increased slowly until the set barely begins to operate, or some fault becomes apparent. If you unplugged the loudspeaker to remove the radio from the cabinet, be sure to plug it in again. You could damage the power supply by operating it without the speaker in the radio circuit.

Another way to protect an old power supply is to make a series light tester. This allows you to place a high-wattage light bulb or a fuse in series with the line to the radio. (See Your Electronics Shop in Chapter 12 for the design of such a tester.) The power supply may not operate with the series bulb, or the voltage may be too low for the rectifier tube to conduct, but you will get some indication of your radio's condition. If the bulb lights to full brightness when you turn the radio on, you have a problem in the primary circuit of the power supply. If the light does not go on at all, you have an open circuit in the primary circuit.

If it lights somewhat dimly, let the set operate that way for a time. You may see a dull glow in the tubes, and you may have enough B voltage for the set to give some indication that it is alive. After you have run this way for 10 or 15 minutes with no problems or odors, you can apply full power. You might replace the bulb with a five-amp screw-in fuse if you can get one.

Beware of high voltage. The power supply of an AC set is designed to handle power at high voltages, which can kill. Be very careful when working in the power supply. If you suspect a problem, use a multitester to check voltages. Touch nothing without knowing its voltage. Never touch any part with one hand while touching the chassis with the other. If you do not own a multitester, get one. (See Chapter 12 for suggestions.)

Fig. 6–1 shows the circuit diagram of a typical AC power supply. Through the years, the insulation in the power transformer of your set may have broken down. Corrosion may have caused voltage divider resistors to open. The filter condensers almost certainly will have dried out and will work poorly. Sometimes these filters regain some of their original filtering capacity after a few minutes of use, but they usually need replacement.

Remember, any unwanted connection between the high-voltage (+) side and the ground of the set will cause the power supply to overheat. The problem may be in the power supply itself, due to an internal short circuit in a filter choke, or, more likely, a bad filter condenser between B+ and ground. The problem also may be caused by a faulty bypass condenser or another part in the receiver.

An excessively high current drawn from the high-voltage power supply will result in overheated transformers or resistors and red-hot rectifier tube plates. The filament of the rectifier should, of course, glow red. The plate is the metal cylinder or casing inside of the glass bulb but separated from the filament. If you see flashing purple or a purple glow in the rectifier tube, it is failing. Turn off your set until you know what is wrong. Chapter 7 on troubleshooting will give you some tips on isolating the problem. Suspect the filter condensers first if you have any problem and replace or test them. If possible check the high voltage (200 to 400 volts) between the positive and negative terminals of each of the filter condensers. If you have good voltage there, the power supply is not short-circuited.

Many of the same points will apply to an

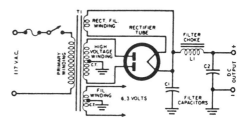

FIG. 6–1 *Typical power supply circuit diagram.*

AC/DC set power supply. Before working with an AC/DC radio outside its cabinet, see AC/DC Receivers in Chapter 7. AC/DC sets can be particularly dangerous.

Looking and Listening

Let's assume that you have powered up your set, and nothing bad is happening in the power supply. Now is the time to use your ears. Put an antenna wire and a ground on your set if it has connections on the chassis marked for antenna and ground, and if it is not equipped with a loop antenna.

Remember, every receiver has three basic sections besides its power source. One is the radio frequency section, which amplifies and selects the wanted R.F. received from the antenna. Next is the detector, which recovers the audio signal from the R.F. transmission. Finally there is the A.F. section, which amplifies the A.F. electrical signal and changes it into audible sound. The largest share of the problems you will encounter likely are in the power and A.F. sections.

After your radio has been on for at least five minutes, turn up the volume control clockwise gradually to full and listen to the loudspeaker. If you do not hear a hiss or a soft hum, something is wrong in the speaker, the audio, or the power sections. Chapter 7 will help you troubleshoot those sections.

If you hear a soft hiss or hum but no stations, even after you tune over the dial, you have trouble in the R.F. or detector sections. The problem also may be caused by low power supply voltages in those sections. Your audio section is probably all right.

If you hear soft static or a weak station, you may have a problem in any section, but the overall condition of the set is not too bad. Check out the audio section by touching the

RCA 1949 model 8X54 brown Bakelite five-tube AC/DC radio.

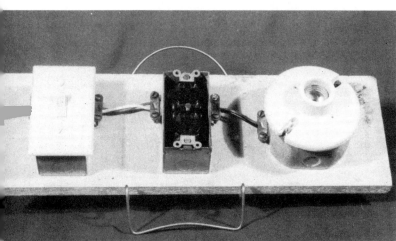

A series light tester, which can be used for trying out a radio.

grid of the first audio tube, usually the second tube back from the loudspeaker, with a screwdriver or your finger. If you are not sure which pin is the grid, you can touch the center of the three terminals on the volume control to get the same result. If the volume control is turned up and the power and audio sections are okay, you will hear a fairly loud buzz.

Once you guess which is the troublesome section in your radio, check the voltages and use the troubleshooting tips in the next chapters to find and fix the problem.

One more obvious problem may emerge. Your set may be making a squealing or loud putt-putt sound. If your set has a regenerative detector, the squeal shows that it is working but is not tuned correctly. More likely such a

squeal results from the loss of some shielding. A putt-putt sound, called motorboating, results from a bad filter or bypass condenser, or a broken connection to or in a volume control.

Once you identify your problems by using this chapter and the next, you can evaluate the nature of the needed repairs. There are several ways to fix the set, depending on its age, value, and the seriousness of its problems. You want to restore the radio, but what exactly does that mean? A look at the different levels of restoration will help you decide which is most practical for you.

Levels of Restoration

Replacement involves putting a modern radio and speaker in an old cabinet. Although a

Motorola 1956 model 66X2 six-tube AC/DC radio in white case with twin speakers.

Zenith 1941 model 6G601M three-way portable six-tube AM radio in luggage case. It is difficult to find straw-colored portables in good condition. This one shows a good deal of wear around the knobs.

Admiral 1947 7RT41-N six-tube AC/DC radio phonograph in large brown Bakelite cabinet with opening top. Admiral made many large Bakelite pieces, including a ten-inch floor-standing TV set.

Zenith 1952 model K515 brown Bakelite five-tube AC/DC clock radio.

RCA 1955 black plastic clock radio with sleep alarm feature.

Sonora 1940 model TV-48 white-painted Bakelite four-tube AC/DC radio with shrimp pink knobs.

good way to rescue an old cabinet, it destroys any value your set may have as an antique radio. Don't do it unless there is nothing that can be done to save the old works, and the cabinet is exceptionally fine.

Modification is changing the actual design of the circuit to incorporate modern concepts. You might modify the circuit to use modern tubes. You might remove an old vibrator power supply and replace it with a modern solid state supply. Most of these modifications are highly technical and would not be tackled by most starting restorers. It is best not to modify an old set. It is all right, however, to use a modern external battery eliminator to run an old battery set, because this involves no modification to the actual radio set.

Functional repair involves replacing faulty components with modern counterparts that perform the same function in the circuit and making no attempt to hide the fact that you have done so. These are probably the easiest sorts of restorations to make. Sometimes when this is done, the old part will be left in place unwired, for appearance's sake, if it shows on top of the chassis. There is a fair chance that the set you restore may already have had such repairs in the past. If your main concern is to have a radio that works, you may want to do what some restorers do: replace all of the paper and electrolytic condensers in the set. This is sometimes called "recaping." Functional re-

pair lowers the value of your set somewhat, especially a classic-era set.

Practical restoration involves making every attempt to make a repair that does not alter the look of the original. New components may be lurking in old cases, but they will look original. Wire, knobs, and other visible parts will be authentic looking, even if they are reproductions. Tubes will not only be of the correct type, but will date from the correct era as well. This is the most practical genuine restoration, and sometimes it is the only possible one. In the interest of the set's history, keep a complete written record of all your work. You may wish to undertake a total restoration in the future, and your records will help you. If the cabinet is refinished in a practical restoration, original-looking finishes and stains must be used.

Total restoration means that only original parts or, if originals are not available, identical modern reproductions may be used. It may take years and several junked radios of the same type to complete a total restoration. It can be a lifetime project.

Most restorers will make functional repairs or do a practical restoration, depending on the worth of the set. But whatever you do, keep careful records of your work. Consider keeping removed parts with restored sets. At some future date, you might upgrade a set from a functional repair to a practical restoration, and the original parts will be useful.

7
Finding the Problem

If you have reached this chapter, you probably have run into some problems. Do not despair!

If you can obtain a circuit diagram for your radio, it will be of help (see Your Electronics Shop, Chapter 12, for assistance). If you do not have a multitester (volt-ohm milliammeter), you probably will want to get one. This chapter and the next will help you understand the various circuits and parts and their problems. We will attack the problem systematically.

It may help you to know the probability of failure of various parts. Service literature estimates that at least two-thirds of all receiver troubles in modern tube-type radios result from tube failure, so this is the first area to check. Of the remaining third of receiver troubles, bypass, filter, tone, and other condensers operating at high voltage account for 12 percent; transformers of all types account for 8 percent; resistors, particularly those operating at high temperatures, for 5 percent; switches for 5 percent; loudspeakers for 2 percent; and miscellaneous for 1 percent.

In radios that have been stored a long time, the failure of condensers and any part subject to corrosion, such as wire-wound resistors, volume controls, and switches, greatly increases. Electrolytic filter condensers will have deteriorated badly, and other paper condensers will have dried out to some degree. Tubes, on the other hand, last a long time because their working parts are contained in a vacuum.

Basic Troubleshooting

When troubleshooting a radio, check the basic voltages first. Even without a circuit diagram,

you can guess what these should be. You have filament or heater voltage if the tubes light. On R.F. amplifier tubes, the plate (B+) voltage is between 45 and 200 volts, with battery sets having the lower voltages. A triode detector usually has a low B+ voltage. On battery sets that voltage may be as low as 22. Audio stages will require B voltages of 67 to 250 volts, with battery sets again having the lower voltage. A circuit diagram will give you more specific information.

If voltages seem close to normal, it is best to start with the last audio stage, prove that it works, and then move stage by stage back toward the antenna. Lacking a tube tester, you still may be able to find a faulty tube in this way. This step in troubleshooting requires some source of signal. In the audio stages an audible signal is needed. Often a screwdriver or a finger touching the control grid will provide enough hum for a test. For R.F. and detector stages, a suitable R.F. signal is needed. Sometimes touching a grid with a bit of metal produces an audible click. It is better to use some regular source of signal, however. Chapter 12, Your Electronics Shop, will help you with the possibilities here.

One particularly annoying problem is the intermittent fault—the radio works only part of the time. When tracking an intermittent fault, note what happens when the set goes bad. Try to guess from the symptoms which section is causing the trouble. Almost any part in a section can cause intermittent operation.

Some intermittent problems are related to heat sensitivity, and trouble appears when the set is warm. Warm your set thoroughly, and trace the problem when it occurs. Often inter-

Radio instruction courses, both resident and (more often) by correspondence, were advertised in radio and science magazines from nearly the beginning of radio. This ad for Coyne Electrical School was seen in Radio-Craft, February 1939.

Triplett 1946 model 2432 R.F. generator.

Westinghouse 1954 model H-397T5 maroon plastic five-tube AC/DC clock radio. A plug on the back allows a coffee maker or other appliance to be plugged in.

mittent problems are vibration-sensitive as well. Try tapping or wiggling the leads. (Swearing at the set may also produce some action.)

Another common cause of intermittent operation is corroded solder joints. These often can be found by examining and wiggling the wires. Once found, the joint can be resoldered. Bad switch contacts can act up intermittently, a common problem in old sets. Working the switch or wiggling its shaft often exposes the fault. Even tubes may give trouble when they are warm. Tapping them often exposes the fault.

An important aid in finding and fixing problems is knowing the problems that accompany different types of receivers. The causes for the problems in each of the following sections are listed in approximate order of frequency, with the first item under each problem the most likely cause, and so on. Not every solution applies to every set, of course, since a particular radio may not have the part mentioned.

Common Problems

PROBLEM: Receiver completely dead.
· Defective tube or tubes.
· Defective power supply. (See following sections on receiver type.)
· Bad tone condenser between plate of output tube and ground.
· Open cathode resistor in power amplifier tube circuit.

· Bad output transformer.
· Bad voice coil in loudspeaker.

PROBLEM: Receiver makes some sound, but no station is received.
· Weak or bad tube, probably in R.F. or detector section.
· Defective filter or bypass condensers reducing B voltage.
· Defective A.F. coupling condenser.
· Oscillator or converter in superheterodyne receiver not functioning properly. Try a new tube.
· Short-circuited tuning condenser. Look for dirt or bent plates. Often radio works over part of dial.
· Tuned circuits out of alignment.
· R.F., I.F., or A.F. transformer open or shorted to ground.
· Open-plate load resistance in audio tube.
· Antenna terminal or coil short-circuited to ground.

PROBLEM: Received stations are weak.
· Check sections noted under the preceding problem.
· Inefficient antenna system.
· Open antenna coil. Try feeding antenna directly to grid of first R.F. tube or mixer.
· Weak magnet in permanent magnet (p.m.) speaker or field coil in electrodynamic speaker.

PROBLEM: Excessive hum.
- Difficulty in power supply. (See receiver type below.)
- Open-control grid circuit in audio stage.
- Cathode to heater short in a tube.
- Bad tube, often a gassy rectifier or output tube, identified by a distinct purple glow in the tube.

PROBLEM: Motorboating (putt-putt sound), or oscillation (squeal), or distorted sound.
- Bad bypass or A.F. coupling condenser.
- Open volume control resistance element.
- Tube shield(s) missing or not making good contact with base.

Battery Receivers

PROBLEM: Radio completely dead. Tubes do not light even with volume control turned up.
- Batteries dead. Check voltages with set turned on.
- Bad wires from the A battery.
- Bad rheostat (volume control). Often the volume in old battery sets was controlled by varying the filament voltage.

PROBLEM: Tubes light but radio produces no sound.
- B voltage is missing. There may be a bad battery or bad wiring from a battery. You may also apply any diagnosis listed under Common Problems when the receiver makes some sound, but no program is received.
- Open grid circuit in A.F. caused by bad C battery. Check the C-battery voltage.

AC Receivers

Beware of high AC and DC voltages in these receivers. Be careful when working inside the chassis.

PROBLEM: Radio completely dead. Tubes do not light even after some time.
- A bad line cord, blown fuse, or bad switch. Open circuit before power transformer.
- Faulty power transformer.

PROBLEM: Tubes light up but radio produces no sound.
- B voltage missing or too low. Remove rectifier tube and check high voltage winding of power transformer. If this is satisfactory, check all parts of power supply. If these are satisfactory, check for defective bypass condensers or a short circuit from B+ to ground.

PROBLEM: Excessive hum.
- Filter condensers that have lost their capacity.
- Short circuit or open circuit in one-half of high voltage winding of power transformer.
- Shorted filter choke or speaker field coil.

PROBLEM: Crackling or sputtering noise.
- Defective transformer or choke winding. The cause may be an arc between a winding and the metal of the transformer. This may be accompanied by a smell of ozone or of scorching. If so, the transformer is ruined. To test, turn off receiver, remove all tubes, including the rectifier, and turn on set. Note if arcing can be seen or a sizzling noise heard. If not, insert rectifier tube (turn off the set to insert the tube, then turn it on) and measure voltage across each half of the high-voltage winding. If the winding is bad, the meter will change voltage when arcing occurs. Each winding may be tested in the same way.
- Defective bleeder resistance. Arcing between the windings of a wire-wound resistor or across a cracked carbon resistor can cause noise. You may be able to see arcs in a darkened room.

AC/DC Receivers

Beware: In many cases the chassis of a low-priced radio is connected to the power line directly or through a resistor and condenser. If the plug is plugged into the wall in one way, the chassis has 115 volts on it and is dangerous. (Remember that nonpolarized plugs were used in antique radios.) If you must work on one of these with the chassis out of the case, use an AC voltmeter to check the voltage from the chassis to a reliable ground. If it reads 115 volts, reverse the plug in the wall and check again. The safest way to work on these sets is by using an isolation transformer (see Chapter 12, Your Electronics Shop). Upon examining Fig. 7–1, you will see that the filaments are connected one right after another, in a series, directly to the wall outlet. In the AC power

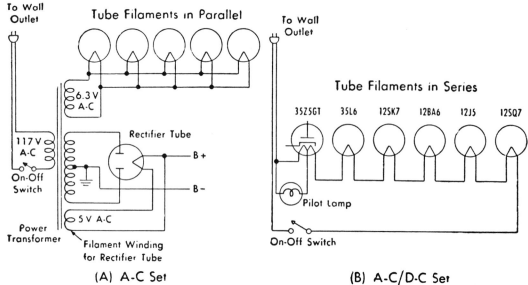

FIG. 7–1 *Parallel filaments isolated from line and AC-DC filaments in series on line (from Markus).*

supply, both the high voltages and the filaments are isolated from the wall outlet.

The B − or ground side of the power supply is likewise connected to one side of the power line. There will be some connection to the chassis for reasons of shielding. This can make the chassis dangerously hot. See Fig. 11–2 for schematic diagram of how this works.

PROBLEM: Radio dead. Tubes and pilot light do not glow.
· Heater of one or more tubes is burned out. Tube heaters are connected in a series, so none will light if one is bad.
· Switch or line cord faulty.

· Defective ballast resistor. Early AC/DC receivers have a resistor in series with the heaters. It may be a power resistor, a resistance tube looking much like a regular tube, or a special line cord with a third resistance wire built in.

PROBLEM: Tubes light but radio does not work.
· Tube is bad.
· B + is low or lacking throughout receiver, exposing a bad power supply. The problem may be a bad rectifier, filter resistor or choke, filter condenser, or shorted bypass condenser.

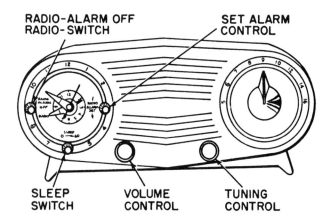

FIG. 7–2 *Typical clock radio layout.*

ANTIQUE RADIO RESTORATION GUIDE

- There is no plate or screen-grid voltage on one tube. Most often this means a faulty I.F. or audio transformer or a bad plate load or screen resistor.

PROBLEM: Pilot lamp does not light but receiver works.
- Bad pilot light. Replace with one with the correct number.
- Bad pilot lamp socket.

Clock Radios

PROBLEM: Radio does not work but clock works.
- The clock switch is not turned on (see Fig. 7–3). The left knob must be turned to radio.
- Any diagnosis of problems of this type in the above sections may apply. Most clock radios are in AC/DC chassis.

PROBLEM: Radio works but clock does not.
- Clock gears plugged with dust. Clean with compressed air and degreaser spray.
- Clock motor has failed. Most of these are sealed Telechron movements that are not repairable. A clock repair shop can get a new movement for a reasonable price.

PROBLEM: Neither clock nor radio work.
- Power not reaching clock. Check wiring to the clock; the radio receives power from the clock.
- Both clock and radio may have the problems listed previously.

Output and Speaker

PROBLEM: No sound, although tubes light and B voltage is normal.
- Faulty speaker. Try another speaker. Any permanent magnet (P.M.) speaker can be used to test another P.M. or field coil speaker. If testing a field coil speaker, leave the field coil connected to the old speaker but shift the voice coil wires. If the new speaker works, check the voice coil leads carefully. Test the voice coil with an ohmmeter; it should have a low but measurable resistance ($\frac{1}{2}$ to 2 ohms). If the set is on and the field coil has electrical power, and you hear a click when you touch the voice coil terminals with your ohmmeter leads, the speaker is good. Chapter 12 shows how to build a test speaker. For repair information, see Chapter 8.
- Open primary winding on output transformer. This will show as no plate voltage on the output audio tube. This can be tested with an ohmmeter (with the power off) or with the test speaker.
- Open or shorted secondary winding on output transformer. If winding is open, it will have high resistance when the speaker is disconnected. If it is shorted, it probably will allow some sound through. A good output transformer will have a primary winding resistance of around 100 ohms and a secondary winding resistance of about one ohm.
- Tone condenser shorted. This will show as low or no voltage on the plate of the output amplifier tube.

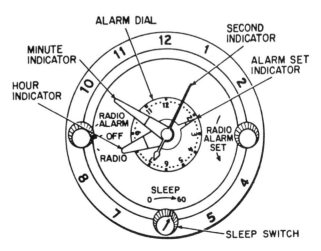

FIG. 7–3 *Clock controls on typical clock radio.*

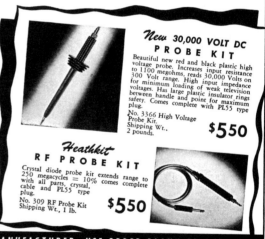
Popular Heathkit vacuum tube voltmeter kit, a very good value in 1951. As seen in Radio-Electronics, *September 1950.*

General Electric 1956 model C415A clock radio with black face on white cabinet.

Motorola 1960 model C4B-1 43 five-tube AC/DC clock radio in two-tone blue and white with gold trim.

Sylvania 1952 model 542CH char-treuse plastic five-tube AC/DC clock radio. Also available with different model numbers in green (542GR), brown (542BR), red (542RE), yellow (542YE), black (541B), mahogany (541M), and ivory (541H) plastic.

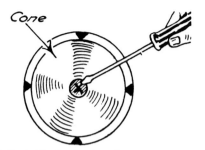

FIG. 7–4 *Testing loudspeaker magnet strength.*

PROBLEM: Weak volume.
· Shorted or open field coil. Test with ohm-meter with radio off. Coil should be several hundred ohms. Test pull of magnet at center of speaker with set on, as in Fig. 7–4. Pull of magnet should be strong. Test with another speaker, following the procedure above for faulty speakers.
· Weak permanent magnet (P.M.) speaker magnet. Test with screwdriver as shown. Try another speaker.
· Partially open voice coil. Try another speaker. Test with ohmmeter.

PROBLEM: Raspy sounds.
· Metal filings or debris in gap where voice coil moves; see Chapter 8.
· Cone warped and off-center; see Chapter 8.

PROBLEM: Rattling sounds.
· Loose cone or center mount. Glue or tape to secure.
· Cone warped and off-center; see Chapter 8.

8
Fixing the Problem

Once you have identified the basic problem with the aid of the previous chapters, you must identify the particular part in the "stage" (the tube or section) of the radio that is giving the trouble.

Beware: Unless you are testing for voltages, all work in the chassis should be done with the power off. No soldering or resistance checking should be done with power on. Test components should be added to a set with the power off. There is only one exception to the power-off rule: when you parallel a condenser or resistor that may be open with a good one, you can touch the wires from the test unit to the wire leads on the one to be checked without touching either lead. (Holding the insulated body of the part is okay.) Having the set powered in this case allows you to hear the difference the new part makes. Before doing a resist-

ance check on a part that may be faulty, disconnect all except one of the wires going to the unit.

The problem of finding replacements can be a test of patience; Chapter 12 will help.

Testing Power Supplies

The largest share of the problems faced are in the power supply, so let us start here.

See Fig. 8-1 for the circuit diagram of a typical AC power supply. Other power supplies are similar, and the AC/DC supply has many of the same difficulties.

Alternating current from the household power line is transformed by the power transformer into the necessary high-voltage AC for the rectifier. It also provides the low voltage necessary to operate the filament of that type

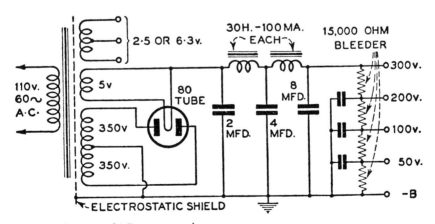

FIG. 8-1 *Circuit diagram of AC power supply.*

80 rectifier, and the voltage necessary for the filaments of other tubes in the set. By taping the high-voltage winding of the power transformer at the center and grounding that center for B−, the alternating current in the high-voltage coil will switch back and forth from +350 volts at the top and −350 volts at the bottom to −350 at the top and +350 at the bottom of the high-voltage winding. Since the rectifier has two plates connected to opposite ends of the winding, one plate is always positive with respect to the filament of the rectifier and draws electrons from the filament (cathode), whereas the other plate, being negative, does not. Thus, one plate draws current at all times. The current drawn from the filament causes the filament of the rectifier to appear positive, for it has a shortage of electrons with respect to the center tap, which is B−.

We now have an electrical current traveling in one direction, since the filament is always positive. We have obtained DC from AC. However, the DC is not even: it has a ripple corresponding to the waveform of the original AC, as can be seen in Fig. 8–2.

This ripple sounds like a 120-hertz hum in the receiver. To eliminate it, add a filter consisting of two or more electrolytic condensers and one or more filter chokes. The power supply illustrated in Fig. 8–2 has two chokes and three condensers. In this high-quality supply, condensers of 2, 4, and 8 mfd. are used with chokes of 30 henrys (H) each. Since these chokes are designed to pass 100 milliamps (ma.) or .1 amperes, we know this is a supply for a rather large receiver. The condenser-choke filter resists variations in the DC applied to it, averages the variations, and gives a smooth output to the B+ lead. Some power supplies use a resistor and higher-capacity condensers instead. Often several condensers are contained in the same case in a radio but are shown separately on the circuit diagram.

The power supply illustrated has another feature not usually found in receiver power supplies—an electrostatic shield in the power

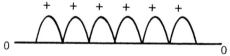

FIG. 8–2 *Power supply ripple (DC).*

transformer. In high-quality equipment, this reduces interference from the AC line. The power supply also is shown with a voltage divider bleeder resistor, splitting the voltage down to 200 volts, 100 volts, and 50 volts for different parts of the receiver. Almost all receivers use voltage dividers to obtain the desired voltage; most diagrams do not show them together like this one does. Note too that the three-voltage taps have their own capacitors (condensers), which bypass audio or radio signals around the power supply to ground to keep them from interfering with each other. Every radio uses such bypass condensers to isolate stages from each other. Because they often start leaking, or passing DC through them, they are a common source of low-voltage or failed power supply.

Now here are the problems: if the B voltages throughout the radio seem low, you need to decide if the problem is in the power supply, or if the radio is demanding more power than the supply can give.

To make that decision, look at a more obvious problem. If there is a noticeable hum in the receiver, you probably have a problem with one of the filter condensers. Sometimes a condenser not only will lose its capacity to filter but also will develop an internal partial short circuit and draw too much power. If one of the condensers becomes warm to the touch, this is likely to be the problem. Test by substituting a good condenser.

If the voltages are okay but there is hum, simply place in the new condenser parallel with the old. The hum should be reduced greatly if the old filter was dried out.

When replacing a filter condenser, remember that high voltage exists on its positive connection. Remember, also, to wire the test condenser with the same polarity (+ to + and − to −). If you wire an electrolytic condenser backwards, it will be destroyed immediately.

Checking the filters will reveal many low-voltage and hum problems. Remember that your test or replacement condenser should have the same or higher capacity and the same or higher working voltage.

A difficult problem to spot is a power supply that does not provide voltage to the set high enough for it to operate properly. It is sometimes hard to know what the B+ voltage should be for the set without a circuit diagram, but it should be well over 100 volts in an AC set, and more than likely in the range of 250 volts.

If the set does not work well, and low voltage seems to be present at the third filter condenser, you need to discover if the problem is in the power supply or in the radio itself. Do this by measuring the voltage at that point and writing it down. Turn off the radio. Disconnect the main B+ wire to the radio and turn on the power supply. The voltage at that point should now be higher than before, but not by more than about 30 percent. If the voltage at this point rises sharply, then something in the radio itself is drawing more current than the power supply can provide.

If this voltage does not rise much and still seems too low—for example, under 200 volts for an AC supply using a power transformer—you have a weak power supply. One cause may be a poor rectifier tube. After long use, rectifiers lose the ability to pass enough electrons to supply sufficient current. The only repair is replacing the tube. If the voltage of the supply seems low when the B+ lead is reconnected to the rest of the radio, check the voltage at the first filter (2 mfd.) and compare it with that at the output of the supply. If your power supply uses a filter choke—a large metal case that looks like a transformer—there should be no more than a 15 to 30 volt drop across it. If the drop is high—60 or more volts—either your receiver is drawing too much current or, less likely, you have a bad filter choke. If the voltage drop across the chokes is very low and the overall voltage to the set is low, the rectifier tube is likely to be at fault.

What if there is no high voltage at all? If you get nothing at the output of the filters, check to see if there is anything at each of the preceding filters. If nothing is there, remove the rectifier tube and measure the AC voltage at the plate pins on the socket. Measure each side to the center tap. The two voltages should be within 10 percent of each other and should be somewhere from 125 to 350 volts AC. If there is no voltage here, check to see if the tubes are lit. If they are lit, there is trouble in the high-voltage winding of the power transformer. If they are not lit, there may be transformer trouble or a problem in the wiring preceding it. Resistance testing, with the plug pulled, should help you find the problem.

You can check the voltage at each winding of the power transformer. If only one is missing, there is a fault in the power transformer. Direct replacements are not easy to find but the fault may not be too bad. Find where the wires go into the transformer. Sometimes they will connect to a metal terminal and break at that point. If there is no break, the transformer may need to be rewound, which is no job for a beginner. It is best to look for a replacement. Although expensive, replacements are available from several sources. You may be able to get one from another old radio with a similar number of tubes. If you suspect a faulty transformer, disconnect the suspected winding completely and check it with the ohmmeter of your multitester. Fig. 8–13 shows the average DC resistance in a good transformer.

If the resistance is much higher—for example, ten times higher—you probably have a bad winding. If a power transformer is bad, a new unit can be substituted if you know the rating of the old one, but your set will be less authentic. Filter chokes also can develop an open winding, since a filter choke is really a transformer with a single winding. If there is no voltage following a filter choke, turn off the power, disconnect one lead, and measure the resistance: it should be somewhere between 15 and 250 ohms. It is a good idea to check the resistance of the transformer and choke windings to ground as well. Center taps on power transformer windings that are connected to ground will have to be disconnected, of course. With the winding completely disconnected, the resistance to ground should be so high as to be almost immeasurable. A faulty filter choke can be replaced with a power resistor of at least five-watt power capacity and about 500 ohms of resistance. Chokes, like transformers, can be rewound.

Some receivers have a selenium rectifier (Fig. 8–3). These usually were used in battery, AC/DC portables. Problems with selenium rectifiers show up as an excessive hum or no B+. They cannot be fixed but they can be replaced with modern silicon diodes of at least 400-volt peak inverse voltage rating and one-amp capacity. Selenium rectifiers are damaged easily when too much current is drawn from them. If the filters are bad in a set with a selenium rectifier, the rectifier likely has been damaged as well.

FIG. 8–3 *Selenium rectifier.*

Triode Amplifier Problems

The reasoning we have used in looking at a power supply applies throughout a radio. If you understand how the section or stage of a set works, you will be able to figure out why it does not work. Let's look at several basic receiver parts to see what is happening.

The key part is the vacuum tube. Essentially, a vacuum tube does one of two things: it rectifies (that is, acts as a one-way valve) or it amplifies (controls the amount of current flowing through it). We have seen how rectification works in our examination of power supply problems.

Let's examine how voltage amplification works in a tube. V1 in Fig. 8–4 is a simple triode tube. For more about triodes, see Chapter 2.

In this circuit condenser, C1 prevents any DC from the previous tube or stage from getting to the grid of V1 and is called a coupling of blocking condenser. The AC signal, shown by the small sine wave above the input, passes through C1 to the grid. When the signal is on the top side of the line, it is positive in voltage and thus causes more electrons to flow from the cathode of V1. If there were no current flowing through V1, the plate would have 200 volts on it. If current flows (because the grid is more positive), current will flow through R3 and the plate of V1; that is, the top side of R3 will have a lower voltage (maybe 170 volts) because of the voltage drop across R3. That is why the larger sine wave of the signal above is the reverse of the input signal, as well as larger. Let's say that the input signal varied from +1 volt to −1 volt and the output varied from +200 to +170. When the input voltage is −1 volts, less or no current will flow, and the plate of V1 will have close to 200 volts on it. A two-volt variation on the input grid (−1 to +1) results in an output variation of 30 volts (+170 to +200). That is an amplification of 15 times. The 30-volt change is passed to the next stage through a coupling condenser. After the condenser, the voltage will measure from zero to +30 volts.

Some necessary parts remain to be examined. Resistor R1 keeps the average voltage on the grid of V1 at ground or zero voltage. It is usually of medium value (around 470,000 ohms) and also prevents a major build-up of extra electrons attracted from the cathode to plate flow in V1. These electrons are drained

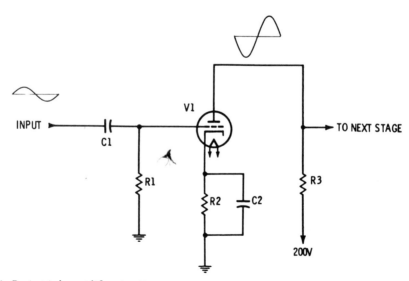

FIG. 8–4 *Basic triode amplifier circuit.*

off through R1, so that it does not become so charged with electrons as to cut off entirely the flow through the tube.

Two things can go wrong with the input to V1. If C1 leaks current from the previous tube (as if it had a parallel resistor), then C1 becomes a voltage divider with R1, and the tube has a positive voltage on the grid, since the left side of C1 has a varying positive voltage. A positive voltage on the V1 grid causes it to conduct too much current and generally causes the tube to operate inefficiently. The usual symptom of a tube that badly distorts is poor sound quality or overheating. The plate in an output power tube may get red hot if the input condenser is leaky. If resistor R1 changes value, some change of sound quality may be noticed, but the tube will operate. If R1 should open—that is, act like it is not there at all—electrons will collect on the grid from the cathode to plate flow, the grid will block, and the tube will not conduct a current. After a while the electrons will leak off and the tube will start to amplify again, only to block a bit later. This leads to the putt-putt sound called motorboating. If this happens to a radio you are trying to fix, look for an open grid resistor. That resistor may be a volume control, but it is connected directly to the grid of the tube.

We also have R2 and C2. When the tube draws current, that current flows through R2 as well as R3. When it flows through R2, which has its other end connected to ground, there is a shortage of electrons at the top of R2 in relation to the bottom of R2. In a typical voltage amplifier the top of R2 might be about +2 volts. Now, notice that the grid is connected to the cathode through R1 and R2, both of which go to ground. The two (and all other) grounds in the circuit are connected. Thus, the cathode is +2 volts if examined from the grid of V1, or the grid is −2 volts (more negative) if examined from the cathode.

Usually you will want the grid to be negative in a class A amplifier. It needs to be negative enough so that the signal input voltage never causes it to go positive with respect to the cathode. In this tube the −2 volt grid voltage is combined with the input signal of −1 to +1 volts, to give us a signal voltage measured from the cathode of the tube of −1 to −3 volts. This is not so negative that it blocks the tube. If R2 should change resistance value, the tube's operation would be affected somewhat. If R2 should open (have infinite resistance), the tube will not operate. The same is true if R3 should open. The condenser C2 is used to allow variations in voltage to flow around R2; it bypasses the changes that follow the signal, so none of the signal is lost across R2. If C2 should short-circuit, the tube will operate inefficiently, and probably will have distortion and sound badly. If C2 should open, the tube's amplification will be somewhat less but will operate normally. Sometimes C2 is omitted entirely from a circuit.

The type of bias used in Fig. 8–4 is called cathode bias and is shown in Fig. 8–5, example B. There are other ways of deriving the necessary negative bias on the tube. Fig. 8–5 example A shows battery, or fixed, bias, which seldom is used in AC-powered sets. Its operation is self-explanatory. Fig. 8–5 example C shows an example of grid leak bias. It works this way: The electron stream from the cathode to the plate causes some electrons to col-

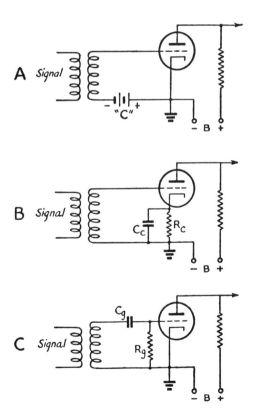

FIG. 8–5 *Tube bias methods (illustration courtesy of American Radio Relay League).*

lect on the grid of the tube. By correctly selecting the value of Rg, we allow them to leak off slowly. Rg is a very high resistance, usually 3 to 10 million ohms. Condenser Cg serves to keep the electrons on the grid while passing the signal from its input transformer to the grid of the tube. Grid leak bias is used seldom in later sets, since it is hard to adjust the bias correctly and the amplifier will have a good deal of distortion. Grid leak detectors are used in simple circuits where distortion is not critical and high sensitivity is important. The bias is set negative enough that the tube cuts off the signal entirely on part of the signal cycle and thus acts much like a rectifier.

Output Amplifier Problems

When you examine Fig. 8–6, you will see how a simple triode amplifier stage is coupled to an output tube, which provides the comparatively high power needed to give volume to the loudspeaker.

The left tube works exactly as it did for Fig. 8–4, except that the grid resistor is replaced by the volume control (R1), acting as a voltage divider to select only a portion of the second detector output. The rest of the tube circuit, consisting of R2, C1, and R3, was explained previously.

The output tube is a tetrode type with two grids (see Chapter 2 for details on tetrodes). C5 couples the output of the triode to the control grid (lower grid) of the output tube on the right. R5 and C2 work for this tube exactly as they do in Fig. 8–4. The second or screen grid is connected to high voltage through resistor R6. Since the screen grid is positively charged, it collects electrons from the cathode to the

plate stream in the tube. That current causes a voltage drop in R6, giving it a somewhat lower voltage than the plate possesses. Condenser C3 is a bypass condenser, which passes the varying part of the voltage across R6 to ground. If R6 is faulty the tube may oscillate (squeal) or be distorted. If C3 is open, the tube will work poorly and may oscillate also. If C3 is shorted (a more common occurrence), then the power supply for B+ will be overloaded and will have a lower voltage than normal or be damaged. R6 may also burn out. Anytime you find a burned resistor, look for nearby condensers that may be bad.

This output tube, like most in small sets, has a tone condenser (C4) that is selected to reduce the high A.F. noise and distortion, producing a more balanced and mellow sound. In most receivers this condenser is connected straight to ground, but in Fig. 6–8 it connects to a tone control variable resistor (R7), which adds resistance in a series with C4 reducing its effectiveness and thus increasing the treble or high end. If C4 should open, the tone will be harsh and irritating. If C4 is connected straight to ground and should short-circuit, there will be no sound, since the output tube's plate voltage will be shorted to ground directly, and the B+ voltage will be low or the power supply may be damaged. The output transformer also may be burned out by the increased current. If you ever have a radio with a burned-out primary winding on the output transformer, the tone condenser is sure to be shorted out.

The last parts in the circuit are the output transformer and the loudspeaker. The output transformer has many more primary than secondary winding turns and reduces the rela-

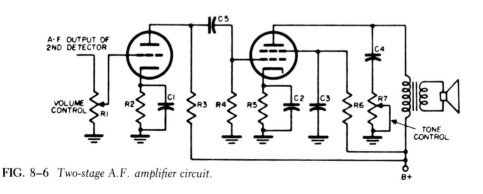

FIG. 8–6 *Two-stage A.F. amplifier circuit.*

tively high signal voltage to the low voltage (at higher current) required by the very light voice coil in the speaker. Output transformers are a frequent source of trouble in receivers because they carry a relatively high current in their primaries. Any transformer that carries a high current in either winding has a high chance of failure.

The speaker turns an electrical signal into movement through the reaction of the changing electrical field to the speaker's magnetic field. That movement moves the cone, which converts the movement into sound waves in the surrounding air. There are many forms of speaker trouble, caused by failure of the small voice coil, by damage to the soft paper cone (usually by mice or mishandling), and by a warped cone (usually caused by moisture), which can lead to its rubbing at the voice coil.

R.F. Amplifier Problems

Fig. 8–7 shows an example of an R.F. pentode amplifier. Very few triode R.F. amplifiers have been used since the development of the tetrode and pentode tubes, little amplification can be obtained from the triode as an R.F. amplifier because of the internal coupling of signals in the tube. Fig. 8–8 shows why. The capacity between the plate and the grid (Cgp) and the grid and the cathode (Cgk), as well as the capacity between the plate and cathode (Cpk), is large enough to cause signal coupling inside the tube itself. Of these internal capaci-

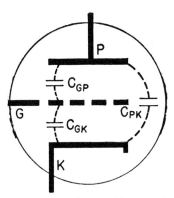

FIG. 8–8 *Interelectrode capacities in a triode tube.*

ties, the Cgp causes the most problems. One type of oscillator circuit, called the tuned plate-tuned grid oscillator, actually uses that internal capacity to make the circuit work.

In the pentode-type tube (see Fig. 8–7), the second or screen grid is second up from the cathode. As far as signal is concerned, it is grounded (through C4). For that reason, it nearly eliminates the effect of Cgp, allowing much more amplification.

The top grid, called the suppressor grid, is quite close to the plate and has the same potential (or voltage) as the cathode. It is rich in electrons and tends to push back into the plate any electrons knocked loose by the intense electron stream flowing through any high-amplification tube. If not suppressed, these electrons will build up a space charge that will reduce the electron flow through the tube.

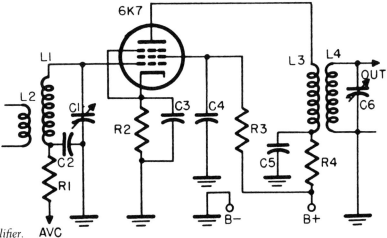

FIG. 8–7 *Typical R.F. amplifier.*

Zenith 1957 model B508R five-tube AC/DC radio in maroon plastic with white front.

Emerson 1947 model 541 five-tube AC/DC radio in wooden cabinet.

Zenith 1951 chassis 5G41 black leatherette portable AM radio. When the cover is flipped, its back side becomes the dial.

Let's see how a pentode R.F. amplifier works. L2 and L1 make up an R.F. transformer, which couples the high-frequency signal from the previous tube or antenna to the control grid of the 6K7. This is usually an air core transformer, although it might have a powdered iron core. Variable condenser C1 tunes L1 to select the frequency desired. Condenser C2 and resistor R1 keep any R.F. signal out of the automatic volume control (AVC) circuit. See Chapter 11 on superheterodyne radios for an explanation of the AVC circuit. It is enough to say here that the AVC changes the negative bias on the 6K7, thereby varying its amplification.

Resistor R2 and condenser C3 provide the basic bias and signal bypassing, the same as the triode amplifier did earlier in this chapter. Resistor R3 sets the correct screen grid voltage for the tube and connects to B+ (high voltage) from the power supply. Condenser C4 bypasses any signal voltage that might collect on the screen grid to ground and works as explained for the tetrode power amplifier above.

The suppressor grid is attached directly to the cathode of the tube (usually inside the tube itself).

The plate of the tube is fed by B+ through the primary winding of the R.F. transformer made up of L3 and L4. The signal is passed from L3 to L4 to the next stage. L4 is tuned to the desired frequency by C6. Some R.F. amplifiers do not use tuned coils so that they can pass the widest possible range of frequencies. Resistor R4 and C5 work as a filter, in the same manner as R1 and C2, to keep any signal out of the B+ power supply circuit. Faults in R.F. amplifiers usually come from failed bypass condensers (C2, C4, and C5 in Fig. 8–7). If these become leaky, they overload the power supply and associated resistors. They also then cease to bypass signals to ground, causing oscillation in the circuit or the failure of the circuit to amplify at all. The condition of the tube is more important in R.F. than in audio circuits and is often the cause of problems. The transformer winding L3, since it is carrying the plate current of the tube, can cause trouble.

I.F. Amplifier Problems

R.F. amplifiers are used a great deal in receivers. The most common R.F. amplifier in old radios is the somewhat specialized I.F. amplifier. Again, see Chapter 11 on receiver theory to understand how this I.F. is developed and used. Fig. 8–9 shows a typical I.F. amplifier. When you look at it, you see a straightforward amplifier of the R.F. type.

As previously noted, vacuum tubes do two things: amplify and rectify. Rectification arises because electrons flow only from the cathode of a tube to a positively charged plate, not in the other direction. In the power supply discussed at the beginning of this chapter, we used this effect to change the AC from the power transformer to the DC the receiver needs to operate.

Fig. 8–10 shows another use for rectification—detecting an R.F. signal. Often called a demodulator, the diode is the detector circuit of choice in most later receivers because it has very low distortion. Its weakness is that it requires a relatively strong signal to work without

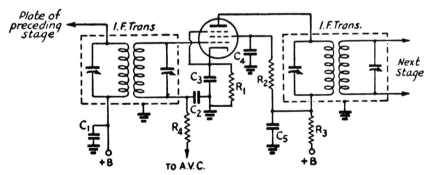

FIG. 8–9 *Typical I.F. amplifier (illustration courtesy of American Radio Relay League).*

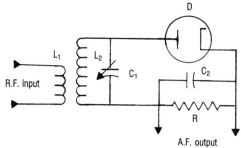

FIG. 8–10 *Simple diode detector circuit.*

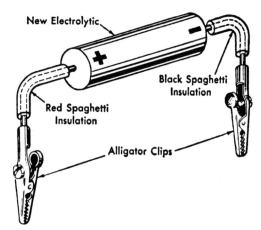

FIG. 8–12 *Useful test electrolytic (from Markus).*

distortion, and it provides no amplification in itself.

Fig. 8–11 shows how it works. A shows the modulated signal as it appears across L2 and therefore the plate of the diode. C1 acts to tune L2 to the desired frequency (in most superheterodynes this is the I.F. frequency). Because the diode conducts only in one direction, current flows from cathode to plate only on the positive half of the cycle. Basically, half the signal in A is chopped off, leaving the rectified R.F. signal shown in B. This signal appears across C2 and R. C2 smooths the voltage according to the average value across it, giving a signal C closely resembling the outside of the varying R.F. signal, which in an AM radio is the audio or sound part of the signal. This signal exists across R and is shown in D of Fig. 8–11. This is the signal that is amplified and becomes the sound we hear. Since voltage levels are relatively low in diode detectors, they are quite reliable. A weak or burned-out tube is the most common form of failure.

Electrolytic Condenser Testing

These condensers appear in power supplies. They also are used in many sets to bypass audio voltages around a resistor and to further smooth B+ between stages in the set, making oscillation less likely.

The best test for an electrolytic condenser is replacement. Fig. 8–12 shows a test condenser you can make up. About 20 mfd. at 350 or 450 volts does well. With the power off, clip across the questionable one to see if the hum is reduced.

These condensers also can be tested with an ohmmeter. Disconnect the positive lead with the set off. Touch the black test lead from the meter to the ground negative side, and touch the red lead to the positive side. The meter will swing sharply toward the zero end of the dial then climb until it reads a high resistance. Several hundred thousand ohms is good. If the resistance remains low, the condenser is leaky. If the meter does not move at all when you touch the red lead to positive, the condenser is open. In either case, replace it.

Transformer and Choke Testing

Several suggestions for testing were given in the section on power supplies. Fig. 8–13 shows the resistances in typical good R.F. and

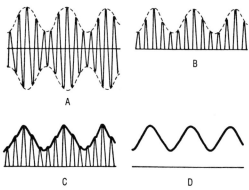

FIG. 8–11 *Waveforms in a receiver.*

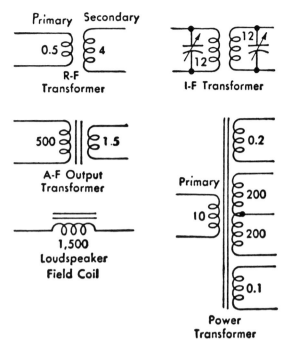

FIG. 8–13 *Average transformer winding resistances (from Markus).*

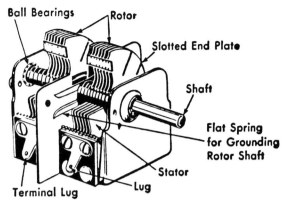

FIG. 8–14 *Two-gang variable condenser (from Markus).*

iron core transformers. Remember to test for short circuits to the case of the transformer with all wires to the windings disconnected. The same sort of test can be carried out on R.F. transformers. Faults will be more likely to appear in the primary winding of R.F. and A.F. transformers than in the secondary winding, because the primary has high voltage and high current flow. Again, any radio part subjected to high current and high voltage is more vulnerable to failure.

If something seems wrong with a transformer, check the emerging wires for shorts to cases or breaks. To solder a wire coming from a transformer, first scrape it clean. It may look like shiny copper, but it is covered with an insulating varnish that must be removed before the solder will stick.

When checking transformers using the resistances in Fig. 8–13, remember that they are only approximate. A circuit diagram for your specific set may give accurate DC resistances. A transformer's resistances may vary a couple of times over from the suggested ones, but the part may still be good.

Tuning Condenser Testing and Repair

If you have carefully cleaned the tuning condenser, the largest problem remaining is that of slightly bent plates, which cause short circuits. If the condenser works over only part of the dial, suspect a short. If you can see nothing touching, disconnect the wire from the stators—the fixed plates usually insulated from the frame. Connect an ohmmeter between the stators and the rotors—the moving plates, which are usually grounded. Slowly rotate the rotor of the condenser from one end to the other. The resistance should be unmeasurably high all the time. Watch the meter as you turn the plates. If the resistance drops sharply, something is shorting the plates. Examine them carefully while shorted, using a good light. You should be able to see the point at which they touch. Clean that point, or carefully bend the touching rotating plate. With a careful touch and patience, you can fix nearly any tuning condenser.

Another problem with tuning condensers is the breaking or corroding of the spring or wire that grounds the rotor to the frame (see Fig. 8–14). This results in poor contact between the rotor and the frame, which leads to noisy or erratic operation. If a wire or spring is broken, fix it with a piece of stranded wire long enough to allow the condenser to rotate over its normal 180-degree range. Use cleaner and fine sandpaper on a corroded contact. Your ohmmeter can tell you if there is a problem

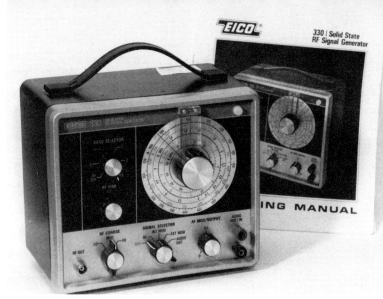

Sentinel circa 1940s model ME-26D/U vacuum tube voltmeter in rugged military construction.

Eico model 330 R.F. signal generator. This is a good general purpose service generator.

here. There should be zero resistance between the rotor and the frame.

Trimmer and Paper Condenser Testing and Repair

Trimmer condensers, with their mica dielectric, seldom cause problems. If trouble is suspected, test them in the same way as you would variable condensers. Usually only a cleaning is necessary.

Paper condensers are far more troublesome. The oiled paper dielectric was not very good to begin with, and age takes a further toll. Fig. 8–15 illustrates some of the ways in which they fail. These condensers, when subjected to high voltages as in bypass, coupling, or tone duty, are vulnerable. There is no way to fix them. For authenticity's sake, open the case of the bad unit and put a modern capacitor inside. Since the modern unit is generally smaller, this can be done.

The beeswax on a paper condenser can be melted off in a low-temperature oven and saved. Place a new capacitor of the same capacity and of equal or higher working voltage in the tube, leaving wires sticking out at the ends, and pour wax into the tube.

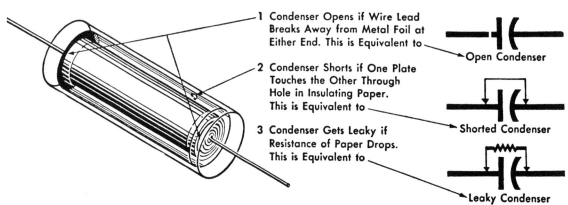

1 Condenser Opens if Wire Lead Breaks Away from Metal Foil at Either End. This is Equivalent to → **Open Condenser**

2 Condenser Shorts if One Plate Touches the Other Through Hole in Insulating Paper. This is Equivalent to → **Shorted Condenser**

3 Condenser Gets Leaky if Resistance of Paper Drops. This is Equivalent to → **Leaky Condenser**

FIG. 8–15 *How condensers fail (from Markus).*

ANTIQUE RADIO RESTORATION GUIDE

Other units mounted in plastic boxes sometimes are sealed with a black substance that can be melted off, but this is a messy job. Some units are in metal cans that can be unsoldered and opened.

The best test for a suspected paper condenser is replacing it in the circuit and seeing if the new one works. It also can be tested with an ohmmeter, following the procedure for testing an electrolytic condenser. Set the ohmmeter to its highest resistance setting. Connect one test lead to one side, and, while watching the meter carefully, touch the other lead to the other condenser wire. The meter will move a little at first but should settle at a resistance of not less than 700,000 ohms. If the meter needle does not move at all, the condenser is probably open. If the resistance is lower than it should be, it is leaky and should be replaced. Again, remember to test condensers with one wire from the condenser disconnected from the radio circuit.

Resistor Testing and Repair

Carbon resistors can change resistance value, especially when they carry much current. Resistances should be plus or minus 10 percent of the marked value, although a variation of 20 percent is often acceptable. Test resistors with an ohmmeter and with one end of the resistor disconnected. Grid leak resistors have a resistance of 5 to 10 million ohms, and only the best meters can measure them. The most successful way to check them is to replace them. If a grid leak tube has an excessively high negative grid voltage and does not work at all, the resistor is probably open. Carbon resistors cannot be repaired. They should be replaced with a resistor within 10 percent of the original value and of equal or greater power capacity. The color code chart in Fig. 4–10 gives resistor values.

Wire-wound resistors can suffer corrosion, burn-out, or broken leads. If a lead burns off at one end, you may be able to unwind one loop and gain enough length to refasten it. If you find a badly burned resistor of any kind, try to isolate what draws current through it and thus has overloaded it. Resistors don't burn by themselves. Check any associated bypass condensers for short circuits.

Volume Control Repair

Volume controls can be cleaned and, on occasion, wire-wound types can be rewound or soldered. Beyond that, not much can be done with them. If a control works but makes a little noise when it is rotated, that is no great problem. If you replace a volume control, remember that the resistance is important, as is the taper, which is the amount of resistance change for a given rotation of the knob. Volume controls that act on the antenna circuit or grid circuit of an audio tube are usually audio taper. Controls that affect the tube filament voltage are linear. Tone controls are usually linear. You can switch the types of tapers around, but if you do, operation will not be as good.

Controls are cleaned, as mentioned earlier, by generously spraying television tuner-cleaner into them and rotating the shaft to move the wiping element of the control back and forth. Often there are small openings behind the terminals into which you can insert the narrow tube from the sprayer. Other times you will have to take off the back of the control to spray the inside. Occasionally the moving wiper in the control can be bent a little to make better contact. Wipe up as much of the cleaner that comes out of the control as possible.

Tube Testing and Replacement

Since vacuum tubes are the most common cause of trouble in old radios, the lack of a tube tester makes it hard to do an efficient repair job. Tubes are available but costly, and you do not want to replace any that aren't bad. Careful troubleshooting often can determine if a particular tube needs replacement. If one tube has a filament that does not light when the others do, it probably has burned out. Even if the filament lights, it may have lost the ability to supply enough electrons to operate well. Something inside the tube may have come loose, and the tube will develop an internal short circuit. If you suspect a tube, check its filament with an ohmmeter. Some battery tubes have filaments so thin that they are nearly impossible to see even when lit, and so delicate that an ohmmeter will burn them out, so be careful with these.

You may be able to get tubes tested at a radio

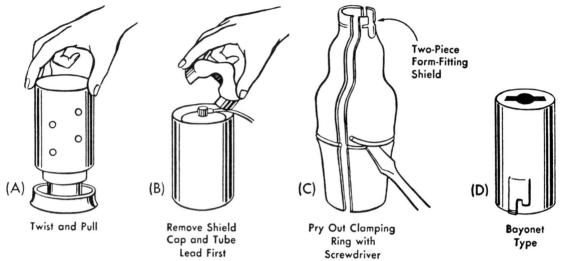

(A) Twist and Pull

(B) Remove Shield Cap and Tube Lead First

Two-Piece Form-Fitting Shield

(C) Pry Out Clamping Ring with Screwdriver

(D) Bayonet Type

FIG. 8–16 *Tube shields and their removal (from Markus).*

shop. A radio shop run by an older person may have an old-style tube tester to accommodate even four-, five-, six-, and seven-pin types. Later eight-pin (octal) and most small miniature tubes can be tested at almost any radio-television shop. Radio buffs in your area may be able to help with tube checking and other problems.

Appendix A gives some of the more common tube base layouts and information about those tubes. For more information consult an old copy of an RCA (or other brand) tube manual.

Another problem with old glass tubes is missing or hard-to-remove metal shields around some of the tubes. Fig. 8–16 shows how these are attached and removed. You can usually tell from the socket if it should have a shield; there generally is a metal ring or clip surrounding the socket and rising a half-inch or so above it. If a shield is missing, the radio may oscillate (squeal) or hum excessively.

Dial Cords and Tuning Mechanism Repair

Most old radios have some way in which the tuning condenser shaft is connected to the dial indicator mechanism. Sometimes even the volume and tone controls have separate indi-

cators. These couplings can give trouble. A metal drive system using washers to transfer the motion of the knob to a celluloid dial often can be cleaned using tuner cleaner. All bearing surfaces can be cleaned and lightly lubricated so that they will move more smoothly, and the whole system can be cleaned up. This will cure most problems with mechanical drive systems.

A large share of more modern receivers, however, use dial cords. Some of these are incredibly complex, using four or five pulleys and three or more separate dial strings, called cords. Dial cord is generally quite thin and is woven around a central core to make a strong, slightly rough miniature rope. New cord can be obtained from a number of sources, such as Antique Electronics Supply in Tempe, Arizona.

If the cord is still there but is slipping, a little rosin on the slipping surface may help. If the cord is frayed or slipping so badly you cannot fix it, make a careful diagram of how it is strung together before taking it apart. Better yet, string the new cord as you unfasten the old. When I am doing this, I use bits of masking tape to hold the cord in place on the various pulleys while I do the whole stringing job. It still isn't fun, but it helps.

If you have a complex dial arrangement and no idea of how it goes together, try to get

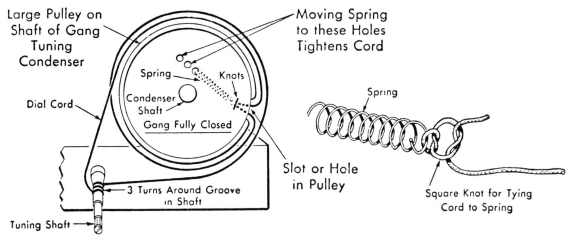

FIG. 8–17 *Dial cord for simple rotary pointer (from Markus).*

service instructions from a Rider or Sams manual. Howard B. Sams wrote a series of small books showing hundreds of dial cord mechanisms listed by radio model numbers. These long-out-of-print manuals are priceless if you repair many old radios.

Included are some diagrams that might help you figure out what you are doing. Fig. 8–17 shows a coupling to a round dial attached to a tuning condenser. This shows how the cord is attached and tensed by a small spring.

Fig. 8–18 shows a variety of typical arrangements to round dials. The one you need may resemble one of these.

Fig. 8–19 gives an example of a simple slide rule scale that spreads the dial out over the top of a radio front. This is a very common arrangement and not too hard to figure out.

Fig. 8–20 shows some examples of more complex slide rule dial systems. If you have something like this but no diagram, you may have to do lots of guessing and experimenting. It is easy to hook these up incorrectly, making the dial go backward.

Finally, Fig. 8–21 illustrates a dial arrangement used by RCA in many of the early radiolas. It is a rugged arrangement using woven metal dial cord. Hard to fix but seldom failing, these systems do well with some cleaning and lubricating.

A number of receivers from the late 1930s and early 1940s use a mechanical pushbutton arrangement that can be baffling. Although

complex, these fortunately are quite well built and usually respond well to cleaning and careful lubricating. Fig. 8–22 shows two of the more common systems.

Loudspeaker Repair

Old loudspeakers suffer from many faults, mainly damage and deterioration of their paper cones. The deterioration takes two forms, warping and breaking. A warped cone has the voice coil at its center rubbing on the center pole piece. This causes a scratchy, distorted sound, sometimes noticeable only when the sound is loud or on bass notes. Fig. 8–23 illustrates how the voice coil fits into the speaker, and how a little warping can cause the problem.

How can it be fixed? Speakers can be reconed, although this means sending them out and spending some money. Your speaker probably will be like the top diagram in Fig. 8–23, with a corrugated paper spider holding the voice coil in the center. This spider is glued in place and cannot be removed.

Here is something you might try, though. First, remove the speaker from the radio, placing it cone-up on a good work surface. Second, remove the dust button or felt in the center of the cone that covers the air gap and voice coil. Third, cut three or four pieces of thick paper or light cardboard about one-quar-

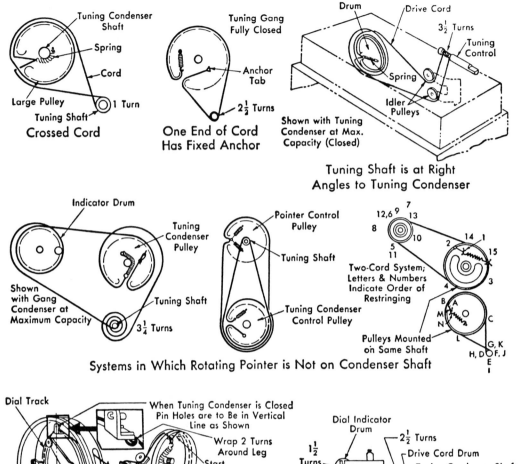

Tuning Condenser Shaft — **Spring** — **Cord** — **Large Pulley** — **Tuning Shaft** — 1 Turn

Crossed Cord

Tuning Gang Fully Closed — **Anchor Tab** — $2\frac{1}{2}$ Turns

One End of Cord Has Fixed Anchor

Drum — **Drive Cord** — $3\frac{1}{2}$ Turns — **Tuning Control** — **Spring** — **Idler Pulleys**

Shown with Tuning Condenser at Max. Capacity (Closed)

Tuning Shaft is at Right Angles to Tuning Condenser

Indicator Drum — **Tuning Condenser Pulley** — **Tuning Shaft** — $3\frac{1}{4}$ Turns

Shown with Gang Condenser at Maximum Capacity

Pointer Control Pulley — **Tuning Shaft** — **Tuning Condenser Control Pulley**

12,6 9 7 13 8 10 5 11 2 14 1 15 4 3

Two-Cord System; Letters & Numbers Indicate Order of Restringing

B A M N L G, K H, D F, J E

Pulleys Mounted on Same Shaft

Systems in Which Rotating Pointer is Not on Condenser Shaft

Dial Track — When Tuning Condenser is Closed Pin Holes are to Be in Vertical Line as Shown — Wrap 2 Turns Around Leg — Start — $1\frac{1}{2}$ Turns on Drum — Direction to Follow When Installing Cord — **Dial Lamp** — **Stop** — $\frac{3}{4}$ Turn Around Dial Track — $3\frac{1}{2}$ Turns — Shown with Tuning Condenser in Full Mesh (Closed)

Elaborate Separate-Dial System

Dial Indicator Drum — $2\frac{1}{2}$ Turns — **Drive Cord Drum** — **Tuning Condenser Shaft** — $1\frac{1}{2}$ Turns — **Pushbutton Mechanism** — **Sector Gear** — View Shown with Condenser Out of Mesh — $4\frac{1}{2}$ Turns Approx. — **Manual Tuning Shaft**

Two-Cord System for Set Having Pushbutton Tuning

FIG. 8–18 *Samples of rotary dial cord systems (from Markus).*

Pointer Clips onto Cord — **Idler Pulley** — **Idler Pulley** — **Drum** — **Tension Spring** — **Drive Cord**

FIG. 8–19 *Simple slide rule dial cord system (from Markus).*

Shown with Tuning Condenser at Maximum Capacity (Fully Closed) — $2\frac{1}{2}$ Turns — **Tuning Shaft**

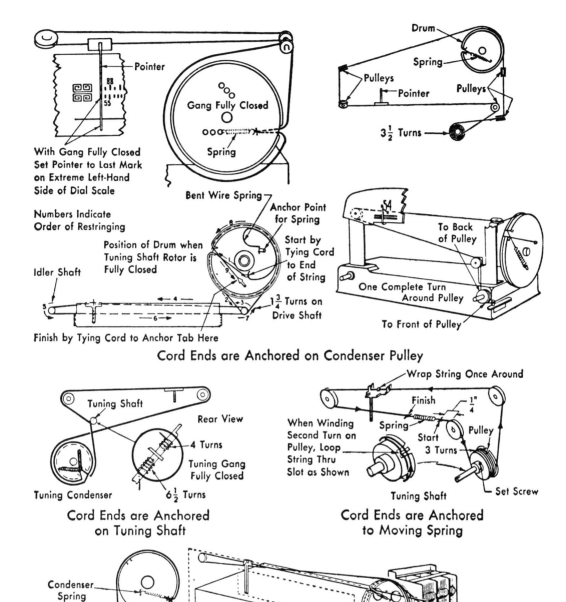

Pointer

Gang Fully Closed

Spring

With Gang Fully Closed
Set Pointer to Last Mark
on Extreme Left-Hand
Side of Dial Scale

Numbers Indicate
Order of Restringing

Drum

Spring

Pulleys

Pointer

Pulleys

$3\frac{1}{2}$ Turns

Bent Wire Spring

Anchor Point
for Spring

Start by
Tying Cord
to End
of String

Position of Drum when
Tuning Shaft Rotor is
Fully Closed

Idler Shaft

$1\frac{3}{4}$ Turns on
Drive Shaft

Finish by Tying Cord to Anchor Tab Here

To Back
of Pulley

One Complete Turn
Around Pulley

To Front of Pulley

Cord Ends are Anchored on Condenser Pulley

Tuning Shaft

Rear View

4 Turns

Tuning Gang
Fully Closed

Tuning Condenser

$6\frac{1}{2}$ Turns

**Cord Ends are Anchored
on Tuning Shaft**

Wrap String Once Around

Finish

$\frac{1}{4}$"

When Winding
Second Turn on
Pulley, Loop
String Thru
Slot as Shown

Spring

Start

3 Turns

Pulley

Tuning Shaft

Set Screw

**Cord Ends are Anchored
to Moving Spring**

Condenser
Spring

OFF-ON SWITCH
AND
TONE CONTROL

VOLUME
CONTROL

BAND SELECTOR
AND
PHONO SWITCH

TUNING
CONTROL

Pointer Spring

Pointer Dial Cord $42\frac{1}{2}$"

Condenser Dial Cord $19\frac{1}{2}$"

$\frac{3}{16}$" Loop

Cable
Clamp

Two-Cord Arrangement

FIG. 8–20 *Complex slide rule dial systems (from Markus).*

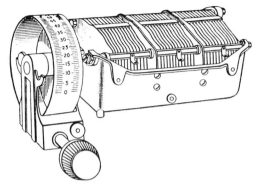

FIG. 8–21 *Tuning system on early Radiolas.*

ter-inch wide and about four inches long. Fourth, slip these between the pole piece and the voice coil, as in Fig. 8–24. They should fit quite tightly. Fifth, spray the cone and voice coil with a fine mist of water so that it is thoroughly wet. Six, set aside the cone to dry thoroughly (at least a day). Finally, remove the shims and test the speaker. If all goes well, much of the warp will have come out of the cone, and the speaker will sound all right again.

You may find that metal filings or dirt have collected in the gap. If so, you will hear a

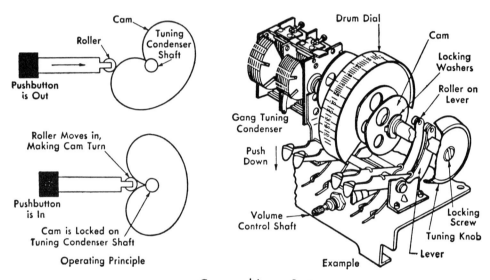

Cam and Lever System

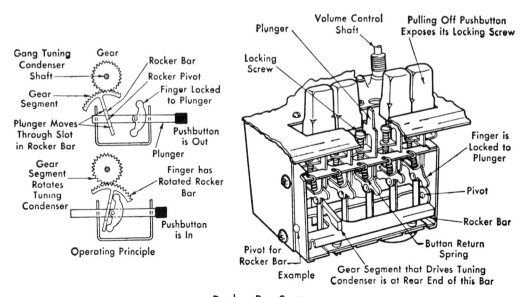

Rocker Bar System

FIG. 8–22 *Mechanical tuning systems (from Markus).*

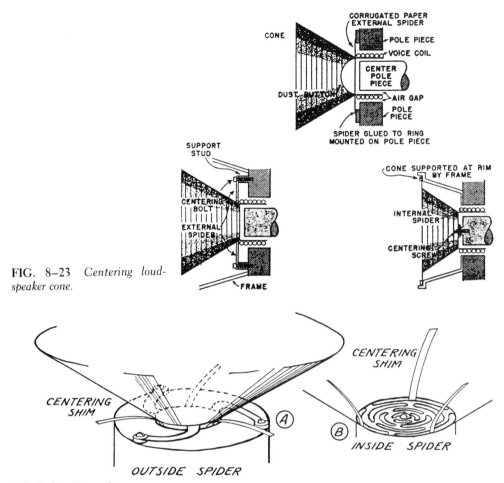

FIG. 8–23 *Centering loud-speaker cone.*

FIG. 8–24 *Using shims to center a cone.*

buzzy or fuzzy sound. Use compressed air and shims to clean out the area. Be careful; the wire used to wind the voice coil is very fine.

Fig. 8–23 shows two other ways the cone can be centered. The spider may be attached to the pole piece in the center with a screw or around the outside with several screws. Fig. 8–25 shows in more detail how such a speaker is constructed. You may be able to realign a rubbing cone in such a speaker by loosening the screw (don't remove it), recentering the voice coil in its gap using homemade shims, and tightening the center screw. Fig. 8–25 shows the cone mounted by screws. Unfortunately, you will seldom find this. Generally the outside of the cone is glued to the frame.

Another common problem is tears or punctures in the cone. You may have caused some

of these yourself by careless handling of the chassis. If a tear is not large, it can be repaired with household cement and tissue paper. You can even try mending tape on small rips, though it may not stick well. As long as the cone is not damaged so that it rubs on the center pole, you can probably improvise a repair. Use common sense.

Another fault that you may not be able to fix is a ruined voice coil. With this fault you will hear no sound. If the coil is open, check the wires leading up to it. Often they are soldered to larger wires and glued at that point to the cone of the speaker for support. That connection can come loose. Careful resoldering is all that is needed. If the coil itself has failed, only a replacement speaker or cone will help.

Older speakers sometimes have field coils

Instruction Book

for the

WESTON MODEL 772, TYPE 6

SUPER SENSITIVE ANALYZER

WESTON ELECTRICAL INSTRUMENT CORPORATION
Newark, N. J., U. S. A.

Cover of instruction booklet for Weston multitester, a well-made, high-grade instrument from the mid-1930s.

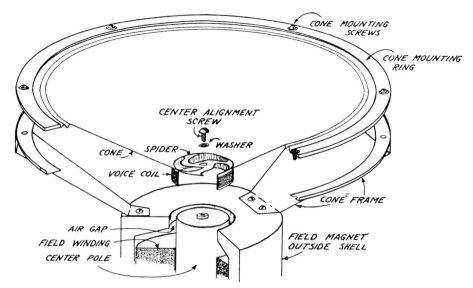

FIG. 8–25 *Construction of a dynamic speaker.*

that may open electrically. A speaker with an open field coil may or may not have faint sound, depending on how the field coil is powered. An open coil shows a high-to-infinite resistance rather than the 500-to-5,000-ohm resistance normal for them. Disassemble the speaker enough to untape the field coil. Often the wire will have failed just inside the tape and can be reattached. If not, the speaker must be replaced or sent away for repair.

Your local Radio Shack store may have a replacement. If you buy one of their speakers, buy the lightest and cheapest in the size you need. Several other sources, like Antique Electronics Supply, also have replacement speakers.

The only speakers sold nowadays are permanent magnet types. You often can replace a field coil speaker with one of these by adding in place of the field coil a power resistor of the same resistance and a 10-to-25-watt capacity. You may have to include more capacity in the filter condensers as well, or the hum may be excessive.

Here are two other tips. First, I never throw away a good speaker. I check to see if it rubs and that it is electrically satisfactory, then I cover the cone with a piece of cardboard secured with masking tape. At that point it can go into storage until you need a replacement.

Second, you can sometimes nest a smaller new speaker inside the cone area of a nonworking old speaker. You may have to fashion some metal brackets to support it firmly, and you may have to cut a piece of stiff cardboard to cover the round space between the new speaker's cone and the old speaker's frame. I have replaced speakers this way without trouble.

Metal Castings Repair

Many early sets have pot-metal castings for switches, variable condenser frames, and even chassis. Deterioration caused by time and poor casting technique often leads to the breaking, warping, or flaking of the metal. While it may be possible to recast simple pieces, repair is more desirable. Epoxy cement glues pot metal well. Pieces may be joined and badly flaking or warping pieces stabilized and rescued by flowing epoxy into the cracks or using it to build up thin spots. This method isn't elegant but it works, and it may in many cases be the only repair available. Some people paint the casting with aluminum paint afterward to cover the cracks and epoxy.

9
Fine-Tuning Your Radio

Superheterodyne Receivers

Now that your radio is working, you want it to work as well as it possibly can. This may require aligning or touching up the adjustment of the internal controls. You'll need an adequate antenna and ground. Most old sets use outside antennas, unlike our sensitive modern radios with their loop-antennas or loop-sticks.

Any adjustment of the trimmer condensers on the chassis or of the tuning condensers should be done with great care. It is easy to make things worse than they are. A safe rule for any person to follow who does not have an R.F. signal generator is, *If it works satisfactorily, leave it alone.* Your set may not work at peak efficiency, but it may be good enough. No harm is done by a nonperfect alignment.

On a superheterodyne receiver, alignment must be done especially carefully. If you are using an R.F. signal generator, follow the instructions that came with the signal generator and also the alignment instructions for your particular radio. An R.F. generator is very useful both for troubleshooting and for alignment. If you do much repair, you will want one; see Chapter 12 for more information. This book speaks only briefly about its use. Consult a more advanced text, particularly on multiband radios, once you are doing detailed alignments.

To do any adjusting, you will need a screwdriver with an insulated tip or, if your receiver needs it, a plastic hex wrench to adjust trimmers and I.F. transformers. Alignment tool sets are inexpensive and helpful. They are available from Radio Shack stores or Antique Electronics Supply.

Lacking a generator, you can make a number of adjustments. The basic rule is to start with the adjustments closest to the speaker. Refer to Fig. 11–2 for a typical superheterodyne. Begin by tuning in a fairly weak station. Keep the volume of your set just loud enough to hear. Start with the secondary of output I.F. transformer between the 12SK7 and 12SQ7. Turn the screw adjustment—visible through one of the holes on the transformer's top—one-half turn. Is the station louder? If so, turn the screw further until the sound begins to get softer. If the sound grew softer when you initially turned the screw, return the screw to the original position and back a half-turn the other way. Find the maximum output. Whenever you turn a trimmer control, turn it only a small distance each time. If adjusting the control seems to make no noticeable difference, put it back where it was originally.

Once you have adjusted the secondary winding of the output I.F., adjust its primary (the other screw) in the same way. Then move back to the input I.F. between the 12SK7 and the 12SA7, adjusting the secondary winding (the rear hole) first and then the primary winding. If the station gets very loud as you adjust, turn down the volume. It is easier to hear changes at low volume. After you have done both, go back and do both again, this time changing settings only a quarter turn.

If you have an R.F. generator, set it to the I.F. frequency of your radio. On most receivers the I.F. frequency is marked on the chassis

WM'S Radio Booster, an antenna tuner designed for the Atwater Kent model 35 receiver. This is a typical radio accessory from the 1920s.

or one of the transformers. In most 1940s and 1950s sets it will be between 455 and 465 kHz. In this radio it is 455 kHz. Connect your generator output to pin 8 of the 12SA7 tube socket through a .1 mfd. condenser. Set radio volume to maximum and the output of the R.F. generator as low as possible for an audible output. Align in the same way as for a station. Using an R.F. generator and an AC voltmeter across the loudspeaker is much more precise than trying to hear a constantly changing station.

After tuning the I.F. transformers, proceed to the R.F. tuning trimmer, sometimes called the antenna trimmer. It is located on the outside of the rear section of the variable condenser and usually is connected to the loop antenna. Tune in a station near 1400 kHz and adjust for maximum volume.

If you use an R.F. generator, adjust it to 1400 kHz, tune the radio to 1400 kHz, and connect the generator to the antenna terminal on the radio if there is one. If there is no antenna terminal, attach a wire to the R.F. generator output, make a loop, and place it next to the loop antenna on the radio. Adjust the R.F. generator for the minimum output you can hear, or measure and then adjust as above.

Now find a station near the bottom of the dial, as close to 600 kHz as possible, to touch up the oscillator trimmer. It is located on the outside of the front section of the variable tuning condenser. If reception is good before you touch the oscillator trimmer, stop. Do not adjust. Changing the oscillator frequency can be a problem, since the dial may be incorrect or the spacing between stations wrong. You may need to adjust the oscillator if you replace the 12SA7 converter tube. If you try, don't forget the original setting, and adjust only if things are not working well.

Again, you can use an R.F. generator in place of a station. Just tune it to 600 kHz and the radio to the same frequency and continue as in the previous section.

Remember, in any adjustment, turn the adjusting screw one-half turn one way. If that increases the volume, keep turning slowly. If it decreases the volume, turn it back, and try the other direction. If you lose reception or hear a squeal, your stage has gone into oscillation, which it should not do. Something is wrong. You can back off the adjustment, but it is better to examine the stage to which the I.F. transformer is connected and try to correct the problem. Tubes are often at fault here.

Also remember that the trimmer condensers may not be in the same locations on the radio you are working on. Use common sense and a circuit diagram if you can get one. Do not adjust anything until you know what it is.

T.R.F. Receivers

On tuned radio frequency receivers (T.R.F.), each R.F. section must be tuned to be in line with the other R.F. sections in the radio. T.R.F. receivers tend to be more sensitive at the high frequency end of the dial than at the low end, so it is best to work in the middle or toward the less-sensitive end. If you have no signal generator, find a station near the middle. Keep the volume fairly low. Start at the stage closest to the detector and tune the trimmer associated with that section of the multisection condenser. It usually is attached to the large condenser it adjusts. Try turning it one-half turn first one way, then the other. Set it for the maximum loudness of the station. Now work back toward the antenna, stage by

Heathkit 1957 model WA2P hi-fi preamplifier (bottom) and model FM3A FM tuner (top) in gold metal cases with gray and brass knobs. These would be used with a power amplifier like the model W-5M or W4-B. Old tube type hi-fi equipment is becoming collectible.

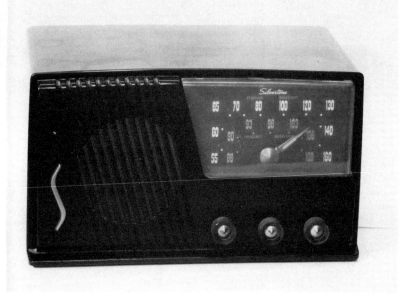

Silvertone 1952 model 57 G 018 brown Bakelite seven-tube AC/DC AM/FM radio. Model 57 G 020 has an ivory case.

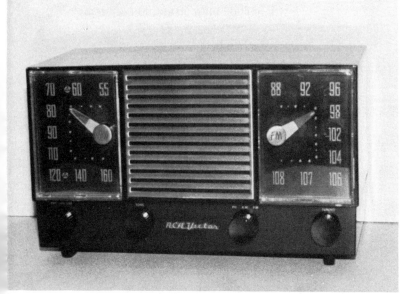

RCA Victor 1953 model 2XF931 brown plastic eight-tube and Selenium rectifier AC/DC AM/FM radio. It looks like a clock radio because the AM and FM dials are separate, but both dials are controlled by a single knob.

stage, adjusting the volume of the radio as needed. You want the most volume without oscillation.

In some sets, no adjustments can be made. Obviously, those sets cannot be fine-tuned. After finishing any alignment job, it is good to go back to the beginning and do it over, making finer adjustments this time.

Again, you can use an R.F. generator instead of a station to make the job easier and the results more precise. T.R.F. receivers do not align as precisely as superheterodynes, so do not expect such good results.

FM Receivers

Working with frequency modulated (FM) superheterodynes is considerably different from working with the AM radios we have been talking about. The I.F. and antenna sections are similar but not identical. The I.F. transformers are adjusted to a considerably higher frequency (10.7 mHz) and are tuned to pass a band of frequencies for maximum fidelity. It is best not to adjust them if you don't have to. Usually they have hex wrench, not screwdriver, adjustments. Remember to use plastic-insulated wrenches and screwdrivers.

It is almost essential to use an R.F. generator and a high-quality voltmeter for adjustments. Sweep generators and oscilloscopes are even more useful.

In AM radios, there are no adjustments in the detector section. FM receivers use a discriminator or ratio detector that must be carefully adjusted for fidelity. If you change one of these, you likely will make things worse.

If you try to adjust the I.F. transformers, make sure you are not adjusting the discriminator or detector. The metal boxes that contain them look much alike.

In servicing FM receivers try to limit your work to tube replacement or repair of power and audio sections. As with AM radios, the largest share of your problems will be in the power and audio sections anyway.

When you work inside an FM set, be careful not to bend the coils even slightly or move any of the wires to the R.F. and I.F. tubes. When you replace a part, locate the new one in exactly the same location as the old.

Antenna Systems

See Fig. 9–1 for one possible antenna arrangement. It is pretty fancy, and you will probably get by with something less complex. Old sets without loop antennas need a substantial antenna system. In general, the higher and longer the antenna, the better, but before you put up an outside antenna, experiment a little. A ground connection to a water pipe and a piece of wire stretched as an antenna near the ceiling of a room may suffice for receiving local stations.

If you are serious about listening, though, you will want an outside antenna. Radio Shack stores sell an antenna package that it calls a short wave antenna that is quite satisfactory. A water pipe makes a good ground. Fig. 9–2 shows a more practical outside installation for most locations.

Antenna systems can attract lightning, so ground them when not in use. A lightning arrestor may be placed between the antenna and its ground, but it is still a good idea to locate a knife switch (available from Radio Shack) inside the window connecting the antenna and ground. When the switch is closed, the antenna will have a direct connection to ground. The only time I leave my antenna ungrounded is when it actually is being used. Never use an outside antenna during an electrical storm. Reception will be poor, and the situation can be dangerous.

You may need to ground your receiver as well. Older battery receivers almost always need to be grounded for good results. AC/DC receivers should *never* be grounded. AC receivers with power transformers may or may not work better with a ground. Try it both ways.

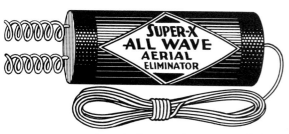

Commercial artist's drawing of an antenna eliminator from 1935. These units usually contained a small loop antenna.

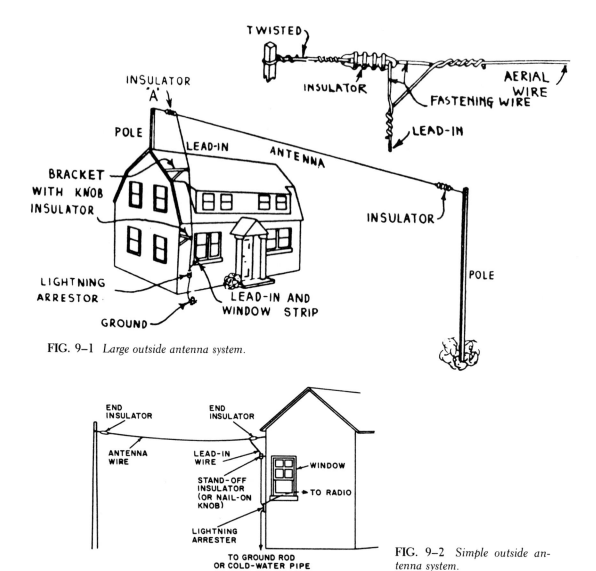

FIG. 9–1 *Large outside antenna system.*

FIG. 9–2 *Simple outside antenna system.*

FM Antennas

FM radios need antennas. An outside antenna gives the best results. The large section of a television antenna works well. In most cases you will use a folded dipole inside the room. Fig. 9–3 shows how one is made and how it comes installed in some FM radios. It is not hard to make one out of some 300 ohm television twin lead.

Many low-priced FM radios simply attach an antenna wire through a very small condenser to the power line. It does not work very well, but it is very cheap. Any of these radios will be improved by putting a simple, hand-made dipole antenna on the wall behind the set. Even low-priced FM radios have connections for an antenna on the back.

Using and Maintaining Your Radio

You fixed your antique radio in order to use it. Still, remember that your old radio, like an antique car, is not up to heavy, day-in and day-out use. Old tubes and old parts will fail in time. They can be replaced or fixed, but repairs can be difficult and expensive.

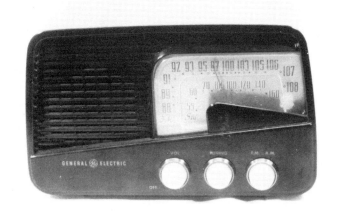

General Electric 1950 model 218 six-tube and selenium rectifier AC/DC AM/FM radio in brown Bakelite with gold dial. Cream knobs are on the right.

Grundig 1958 model 97 seven-tube AC AM/FM/shortwave radio in maroon plastic with ivory and gold trim. German made with European styling.

RCA 1939 model VA-20 brown Bakelite phonograph with wireless phono attachment for a radio. It has a small built-in transmitter to be picked up by a radio.

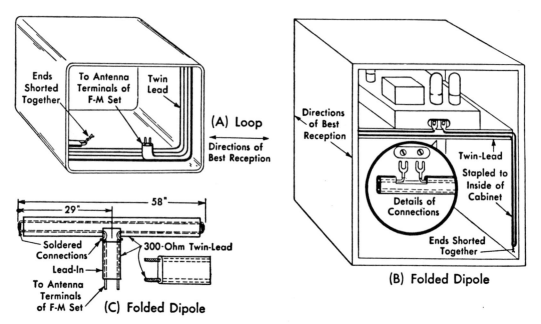

FIG. 9–3 *Typical FM antenna installations.*

Remember, too, that your old radio probably will not be as sensitive or sound as good as a modern set, partly because of its age and partly because newer sets use improved technology.

However, it is good to use your old radio regularly. Filter condensers will stay in better shape, controls will not get stiff or freeze on their shafts, and you will spot problems early, when they can be fixed easily. About an hour a week of use will help keep your radio healthy. (It is nice to be able to brag a little, too: "I was listening to Chicago last night on my 50-year-old radio, and . . . .")

Keep it clean, too. Old wooden cabinets benefit from polishing with a soft cloth and turpentine. Paste wax works well on plastic cabinets. Wax can be used sparingly on wooden cabinets as well. Every couple of years, you may want to take the chassis out of its case and clean it again, as you did when you first brought it home.

Use your radio with sense, take care of it, and get to know its personality. You are preserving a valuable piece of history. It probably won't make you rich, but it will give you a lot of satisfaction.

10
Cabinet Repair and
Refinishing

Wooden Cabinets

With the radio working well, the question arises of what to do with the cabinet. The rule is: the less you do to the cabinet, the better. Antiques and collectibles are expected to have a patina, resulting from the normal wear and tear of age. Small scratches and wear areas are to be expected after 30 or more years of use.

The finish actually may be better than you think. That's why the first step is to clean the cabinet thoroughly. Even though a patina is acceptable, dirt and grime are not.

Use mineral spirits. Other solvents (alcohol or lacquer thinner, for instance) can dissolve the finish and leave you with a stripping job instead of a simple clean-up. Even if you plan to strip off the finish later, start with this clean-up. You may find that it's all you need.

In addition to mineral spirits, you will need to have a lot of 3/0 steel wool on hand. Also have a large supply of clean rags.

Unwind a portion of the steel wool roll and pull off enough to make a comfortable pad. Steel wool can shed metal specks, so be careful. Wearing heavy rubber gloves will help avoid getting a small, difficult-to-remove metal slivers in your fingers. Have the rags cut into one-foot-square pieces; this size allows you enough material so that you can shift the rag to a clean area.

Apply the solvent to a small section of the cabinet (about one square foot) at a time. Taking a pad of steel wool, rub gently with the grain, back and forth in straight lines. Leaning too hard on the pad results in scratches where your fingers apply the pressure. Take a clean rag and wipe up the residue. Keep turning the rag to use a clean section, or you will just redistribute the dirt instead of remove it.

Remove the knobs to clean underneath them. The area around the knobs is likely to be among the dirtiest, and trying to clean without taking off the knobs often leaves a dark, dirty circle around them. Don't forget to clean the edges of the cabinet as well as the flat parts. They often have lots of fingerprints on them. Once the main portion of the cabinet is cleaned, this remaining dirt will look worse than ever.

When the radio is clean, examine the finish. If it has a good but dull finish, restore the shine. Don't worry about the small nicks and wear areas; these are part of its history. Use a good paste wax or a good-quality furniture wax, a soft rag, and lots of elbow grease to produce a good shine. Dampen the cloth, put a chunk of wax in the center, screw up the ends, and rub the pad in a circular motion over a small area. (Always work on small areas. If you attempt too large a section, the wax will dry and make your polishing job much more difficult.) Apply a light coat. Finish by rubbing with the grain. Depending on how strong your arm is, you can wait one to three minutes to buff the wax out. The instructions with one commercial wax say it should dry to a haze. If it dries harder than that, it takes a lot of rubbing to get a shine. Use a soft lint-free rag and rub hard with the grain. Repeat coats may be necessary to get the shine you want. Do not attempt to cut corners by putting on a heavy coat. Several light coats are much better.

Do not put anything on top of the newly

Clarion Jr. (Transformer Corporation of America) 1933 model 320 five-tube AC upright table radio, typical of the 1930s.

Crosley 1941 model 25AW seven-tube AC AM/SW/ police band table radio with push buttons and vertical walnut-color wooden cabinet.

Zenith 1936 model 6S229 upright walnut six-tube AC table radio with AM and two shortwave bands.

Zenith 1951 model H503 five-tube and selenium rectifier three-way portable radio covered in brown alligator fabric.

waxed finish for 24 hours, as it needs time to harden.

Refinisher or Stripper?

If the cabinet has a bad finish or has been painted, you may decide the cabinet has to be refinished or stripped. There are major differences between refinishers and strippers. Refinishing removes the finish and requires a lot more effort than stripping, but it doesn't affect the stain originally applied to the wood. All it does is take off the finish. Strippers remove everything down to the wood itself. If the radio has been painted, you must use a stripper. If it has a clear finish, use a refinisher. Refinishers are gentler to the wood and leave its natural discolorations. In either case, try to keep either substance from running into areas that are not going to be refinished, like the bottom or the insides. A professional job doesn't leave streaks of stripper or refinisher in unwanted places.

Take time to examine the cabinet carefully. Check the condition of the veneer, especially if it is decorative. Select a method that will treat the veneer as kindly as possible.

Companies sometimes used a paper veneer. A wood grain pattern was printed on thin paper and glued to the cabinet as trim. It was a cheap way of producing a fancy burl or an exotic wood look. It is obvious upon careful examination. The paper veneer is slightly raised above the surface of the wood, instead of being the same height, with a visible line showing the join. Examination with a magnifying glass will show the halftone printing method used to produce the fake veneer.

Do not use a stripper on this veneer or you will ruin it. Experiment carefully if you use refinisher, and use as little as possible on this paper trim.

Before you start to work, take the chassis out of the cabinet. Keep all knobs, screws, and any other loose parts in a safe place. Label everything so you can get the pieces back where they belong. Protect whatever paper labels are still on the cabinet by fastening a piece of plastic over them. Since you won't be stripping the inside of the cabinet or the bottom, this will keep any spatters away from the labels. When you finish the set, remove the plastic.

Using Refinishers

Many brands of refinishers are available in hardware stores. People develop their own preferences and swear that one brand is better than another. Try one and see how it works. If you find that the one you buy isn't satisfactory, try another brand. They all require lots of rubbing. Whichever brand you buy, read the directions carefully. Then read them a second time, in case you missed something. If you have questions, the manufacturer can tell you what it found to be the most efficient method of using its product. With the current interest in disposing of toxic wastes, the directions should tell you if you need to do something special with the leftovers.

Some rules apply to all refinishers. Wear protective goggles in case something spatters. Use protective gloves on your hands. Use refinishers outdoors, preferably, to avoid the fumes. Even outdoors, don't stick your head right down next to the work, as the fumes are poisonous. Work in the shade, and don't work in drafts or stong winds. This causes the solvents to evaporate too rapidly. The faster they evaporate, the more you have to use, and that's expensive. Work in temperatures above 65 degrees Fahrenheit. Do not use refinishers near open flames.

If you use refinishers in the house, be sure to have good ventilation. Open windows and provide for cross-ventilation. Since you don't want to waste refinisher through evaporation, put yourself in the draft and your work just outside of it.

Pour about two cups of refinisher each into two metal or glass containers. Cap the refinisher can immediately. Divide a pad of 3/0 steel wool into three or four pieces. Be sure to wear rubber gloves. Wet the steel wool in refinisher, squeezing it until it is damp but not dripping. Apply it to an area the size of a plate and rub in a circular pattern. When the finish starts melting and the pad begins to gum up, rinse the pad in the second container. This removes much of the sludge and keeps you from redistributing it on the clean surface. Then go back to the first container and repeat the process. Use a clean rag to wipe up the area and remove more finish. When the refinisher becomes thick and sludgy, pour it into another tightly covered jar until you're done with the project. (You can reclaim some of the refinisher for another project by allowing the used refinisher to stand. When the residue settles to the bottom, pour off the clean refinisher and use it again.) Add refinisher to the two containers as necessary. Change steel wool pads whenever they become filled with sludge. Don't use rags when they become dirty.

When one area is clear of finish, move on to another, remembering to overlap the previous area. When the entire cabinet is clean, go over it a second time with clean refinisher and a clean pad to remove any remaining finish. Keep your steel wool pads clean for this final cleaning. Allow the cabinet to dry for an hour. Buff the entire surface lightly but thoroughly with 4/0 steel wool. Now it's ready for its new finish.

Using Strippers

If the radio has been painted, you will have to use a paint stripper. In the past, strippers had a methylene chloride base, which is highly toxic. Anything said about care in using refinishers applies twice as much to strippers. New strippers that claim to have removed many of these problems have been introduced lately. The first we found was 3M's Safest Stripper. With our new concerns about health and the environment, more of these improved strippers will become available.

They have less harmful fumes and can be used indoors or out. However, they are inflammable. They work slowly but have a long active time, up to 30 hours, letting you work them more easily into your schedule. There are some drawbacks, however. They can cause eye irritation, so eye protection should always be worn in case of spatters. These products should be stored carefully out of the way of children and pets. Despite their safety claims, it is probably a good idea to work with protective gloves. Since they are water based, they may be harder on veneers than methylene chloride strippers or refinishers. They are also relatively expensive.

Whatever disadvantages they have are minimal compared with the hazards of using the older strippers. There is no reason for taking chances with your health.

Because these are so new, read the directions very carefully and buy any related products that the company requires. Safest Stripper, for instance, warns against using steel wool for clean-up because it may cause dark spots. Follow the directions exactly; if you've done stripping before, your old techniques may no longer work. Do remember to wear eye protection, gloves, and old clothes.

If there are doors on the cabinet, take them off. They're easier to strip lying flat. Remember to label the screws and put them with the knobs and other hardware from the radio. One theory about where to start on a piece of furniture is to take the most complicated section and do it first. If there is carving on the front that will require using a toothbrush to get the stripper out of the corners, begin with that. Keep stripping the more difficult sections, working your way to the easiest one. This way, the most difficult work is done while you still have some ambition. Other people prefer starting at the top and moving methodically down to the sides and finishing with the front. Do whatever works for you. Make it as easy for yourself as possible, so that you don't leave the radio half-done because you ran out of enthusiasm.

Don't use putty knives to get residue out of corners and carvings. It is better to use brass brushes, tongue depressors, toothbrushes, and toothpicks for getting sludge out of cracks. A good stripping job must remove residue in the crevices. It takes patience to do the job right. For the last bits of residue that absolutely won't come out, try cotton swabs or toothpicks dampened in lacquer thinner (a volatile solvent, so don't use it with poor ventilation).

After the stripper is removed, go over the entire cabinet with mineral spirits and clean rags. All the finish is gone now, but so is the original stain. At this point you may be shocked to find that the wood, which you assumed would be walnut underneath the paint, is a hodgepodge. When the manufacturers used clear dark finishes, they could use many different woods in the radio, because the colored finish would make them all look alike.

Let the cabinet dry at least 24 hours before staining or finishing it.

Staining and Varnishing

If you have used refinisher, a light sanding with 150-grit sandpaper may be all that is necessary, so proceed to the next section, on varnishing. If you have stripped the radio, read on.

Before any staining or varnishing can be done, the wood will have to be sanded. Use a

RCA Victor 1941 model 35X six-tube AC/DC radio. Note the Nipper design on the right side of the dial.

Philco 1940 Transitone model PT-44 five-tube AC/DC radio. This has an interesting cabinet, especially with the lyre back, which is made of wood.

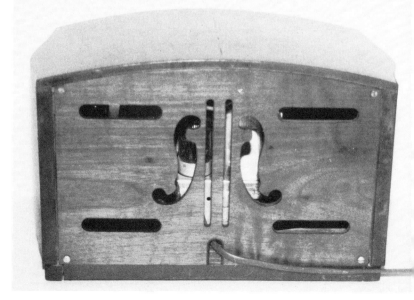

sanding block to give a smooth finish. Always sand with the grain, and be careful not to put any weight on the block as you reach the edges. Radios are veneered, and it's much too easy to sand right through the veneer as you go off the edge. Work your way upward in sandpaper numbers. Starting with 100-grit, go lightly over the surface with the grain, trying not to sand more in one area than another. It will be necessary to work into corners using a folded piece of sandpaper and a finger. Rub gently with the grain in these hard-to-reach places. Don't try to speed things up by sanding across the grain; it will take you ten times longer to sand out those scratch marks than to avoid them in the beginning. Wipe off the surface with a lintless rag and mineral spirits. If you don't use a lintless rag, tiny specks of lint will catch in the wood grain and only can be removed one at a time with a fingernail.

Repeat this whole process using 120-grit sandpaper. If you're staining the radio, stop here. A smoother surface will have a harder time taking stain. If you're planning on a clear finish (no stain) or painting the radio (and that was sometimes done, even by the manufacturers), go over the whole thing again with 150-grit. For an even smoother finish, do this again with 180-grit sandpaper, and even 220-grit. Use each grit in order; do not skip. Remember to do the mineral spirits wipe-down each time.

Once the cabinet is down to bare wood and sanded, the choice of stains, fillers, and varnishes is yours. Again, whatever you use, read the directions carefully.

If you wish to fill the grain so the surface is flat and smooth, buy paste wood filler in walnut, mahogany, or natural. Many radio cabinets have an extremely smooth finish. Their manufacturers used filler to give this flat surface. Fillers are applied heavily to the surface, then wiped off against the grain with a burlap-type rag. Read the directions on the can to do the job right. It's important to follow these directions to get the best results.

Many people skip fillers, desiring a more natural wood look. They rely on the varnish to help smooth out the surface without making it look artificial. Some people also prefer not to stain the cabinet.

In most cases, though, you will want to stain it. This will even out the color of the wood. In the case of many different woods on a piece, staining is almost a necessity. It won't make all the woods the same, but it will help to give them all the same color tone.

Stains may be water based or oil based, runny or gelled. Probably the easiest, most forgiving stain to use is a gelled stain or a pigmented wiping stain. Follow the directions on the can exactly. In most cases, you rub on these stains with 3/0 steel wool. Use a soft, lintless rag to wipe it up. Do not use diapers or T-shirts, they're soft but not lintless. There's nothing more infuriating than finding little white lint specks in your nice stain job. They also tend to wick away some of the color, making it less uniform. Use a stain darker than the result you want. Wipe it on, let it remain for ten to fifteen minutes, then gently wipe off the remaining stain with a soft, lintless rag. Wipe off as much as you want, as you have some control over the final color. After using a gelled stain, wait at least 72 hours before applying a finish coat.

Sometimes the color looks artificially flat, without much variation. The simplest way of correcting this is to wipe on a darker stain, such as walnut over oak or mahogany, and immediately to wipe it off against the grain.

When varnishing, use new varnish. Old varnish may not dry well.

A wipe-on varnish finish is applied with a cloth rather than a paintbrush. If you wish to brush on varnish, read on. The wipe-on finish requires more coats than brush-applied varnish, but it is less subject to mistakes. It doesn't take long to do it each time. Use either a satin or gloss varnish, not polyurethane varnish. Anything you do to the cabinet should be reversible (if necessary) by someone else. At present, polyurethane varnish is extremely difficult to remove and should be avoided for collectibles.

If the radio is still too light, too bright, or too multicolored after staining, use a colored varnish for the first coat or coats to help even up the color. A light coat of walnut-colored varnish will soften the red of a mahogany stain. A dark walnut varnish will help cover the birch/walnut/ash base of a cabinet originally dark brown.

Before applying the varnish, wipe the entire cabinet with a tack rag (available in paint departments) or a lintless rag dampened with

DeLuxe circa 1933 unknown model radio. The radio was made for DeLuxe (as well as other companies) by an unknown manufacturer.

Philco 1952 model 52-542 black Bakelite radio. This is the same radio as the 1951 model, but it has a much less attractive cabinet.

Philco 1951 model 51-542 black Bakelite five-tube AC/DC radio with clear grille and silver color grille cloth with clear knobs.

mineral spirits. Wait for the radio to dry. Cut a piece of lintless cloth large enough to make a comfortable pad in your hand. Before you start on the radio, try this technique on a scrap piece of wood. What you're attempting to find is whether you have to thin the varnish before using it. If you find the varnish is thick before you go back to wipe it up, thin it with a small quantity of mineral spirits. If your pickup rag drags on the varnish, the varnish is too thick.

Pour some of the varnish into a pan (throw-away aluminum pie pans are excellent) and recover the varnish can immediately. Dampen the rag in the varnish and wipe it over a small area on the surface of the wood. Work from the top of the radio to the bottom. When you complete wiping on the varnish in a section (like half a top, or a portion of the side), use the same cloth to wipe off excess varnish. Wipe in the direction of the grain. There should be no wet-looking spots. Continue until all of the cabinet is finished. If you plan to do this outside, pick a still day to keep stray dust motes from landing on your work.

Let the cabinet dry at least overnight. One advantage of the new varnish is that the drying time is shorter. When it is no longer tacky (if you wonder if it's still tacky, it probably is, so wait longer), sand very lightly with the grain with 600-grit sandpaper. This is a once-over-lightly sanding, a lick-and-a-promise type. It is simply slicking down any slight specks that may have landed.

Reapply the varnish as many times as necessary, until you get a finish you like. It probably will require five to ten coats. This takes time, but it is easy to do.

If you're varnishing with a brush, be careful of air bubbles. Do not stroke the brush back and forth; move it only in one direction. Start at one edge, applying two brush widths of varnish against the grain. Then with the grain, brush over these two widths and across a third (varnish was not applied to this one). Continue to work across the pieces, always leaving one space followed by two varnish-filled brush widths. Do your brushing toward the completed section. Brushing across the varnish and into the empty space leaves the brush finishing in the previously completed area. Always finish a section by lightly using the tips of the bristles, brushing the section just completed into the previously finished section. This

method will keep one section from being thicker than another. The final stroking is always with the grain.

When the varnish is dry (and give it plenty of time), use the same sanding techniques discussed in the section on wipe-on finishes. Usually two coats of varnish are enough.

When the finish is completely dry, it should be waxed. You may want to use one of the colored waxes, such as Briwax or Minwax, to deepen the color a bit and take away some of that just-varnished look. Do some experimenting with waxes; you can always remove them with mineral spirits. Allow 24 hours for the wax to dry completely.

Veneer Replacement

Veneer should be replaced before refinishing the cabinet but after staining. Replacing veneer is a cut-and-try project. Trim out the rough veneer around the missing section with a sharp knife, making a smooth-edged pattern that can be transferred later to your replacement veneer. Match stains, making sure to stain a large enough piece of veneer so that you can cut several pieces if needed to get a good fit.

Straight edges are easier to match than curved ones, but don't make a perfect square or the join will be obvious. Angled lines are easier to overlook, so parallelograms, trapezoids, and other angled patches are best. Lay a piece of thin paper over the missing veneer and, as carefully as you can, trace around it with a sharp pencil. Cut this pattern and lay it in the hole to see where it is wrong. If your pattern is too large, trim it down to size. If it's too small, make another, larger one. Cut and try until you have a good fit. It's easier to experiment on paper than on veneer.

Cut the veneer, remembering to keep the grains going in the same direction and to match the style of grain as closely as possible. If you're lucky, the piece of veneer will fit on the first try. If it doesn't, trim it or cut another slightly larger piece.

Use white glue to install the veneer. If you have clamps or straps, use them. It's important to snug the veneer tightly to get a flush top surface with no cracks around the replacement. If you don't have clamps, make simple ones using two books, plastic wrap, and some

RCA 1950 model BX-6 five-tube and selenium rectifier three-way portable radio with an interesting aluminum case.

RCA 1955 model 4X551 black plastic five-tube AC/DC radio, an interesting design with the tuning knob on top.

Stewart Warner 1954 model 9170J four-tube and selenium rectifier three-way portable radio in red plastic.

strong cord. Lay the plastic wrap over the veneer, making sure no glue is seeping out. Hold a book over the patch, put the other book on the opposite side of the cabinet, and have someone else pull the cord tightly around the entire project and tie a firm knot. Twist a stick in the cord to tighten, as in applying a tourniquet. This should apply pressure on the patch while preventing the cord from digging into the wood on the other side of the radio. Leave overnight before unfastening.

Old veneer always matches better than new veneer. Keep old pieces in case you need them some other time.

Grille Cloth Repair

If grille cloth is in good condition, you're lucky. Leave it alone. If it is very thin and showing wear or rips, repair the original cloth if possible. Use a thin, neutral-colored fabric, like silk. Make a sandwich: put Stitch Witchery, or some other interfacing that fuses two pieces of fabric together, in between the grille cloth (front side down) and the silk. Be sure there are no wrinkles. If there are loose threads in the speaker cloth, place them as smoothly parallel as possible. Follow the directions for the fusible interfacing. Most directions require that you set your iron at wool, place a damp press cloth over the piece to be fused, and press with a stationary iron on each area for ten seconds. When cool, place the sandwich in the radio. It will look original. Sound transfer will be reduced slightly but not seriously.

If the grille cloth is hopeless or missing, replacement cloth is available from Antique Electronics Supply. It offers enough of a variety to allow a good if not perfect match.

Plastic Cabinets

A different technique is required to refurbish a plastic cabinet. Since water does not damage plastic, clean-up starts with soap and water. Protect whatever labels are on the bottom or inside the cabinet. If the label is in bad condition, clear packaging tape will cover it and keep the bits and pieces from further deterioration. In this case, the plastic will stay on the set even when it is finished. If the label is in good

condition, cover it with a piece of plastic taped around the outside to keep water out. Remove this when you are done.

Use liquid soap and a rag. Carefully wash inside and out, removing as much dirt as possible. The visible surfaces can be scrubbed vigorously after you have removed any grit with a gentle washing. Use a soft toothbrush to clean the corners and louvers. Do not use steel wool, scouring pads, or any other abrasive substance. These will leave scratches that are virtually impossible to remove. A soft rag and elbow grease is safer. The same cleaning approach is good for painted plastic cabinets. Be careful of too-vigorous scrubbing on painted cabinets, though. Always remember: Don't do more than needed to get it clean.

For really bad cabinets, like the ones that have spent years in the barn, start with a simple water wash to clean off the loose stuff. Then use a foaming tub and tile cleaner to cut through the grime. Do not do this on painted surfaces or on a cabinet that still has some shine, as there's a good chance it may dull the finish. Some restorers refuse to use a cleaner like this, but I find it works well on the difficult cabinets. It is always the technique of last resort. You will have to do a lot of polishing when you are done.

There are as many opinions about polishes as there are polishes in the world. Everyone seems to find one that works well for them. If it works and doesn't damage the radio, it's fine. Here is one suggestion.

Use a brass polish (such as Brasso or Wright's). Follow the directions carefully. Using only soft rags, rub the polish on. Keep rubbing as long as the polish is wet. It is not necessary to apply a lot of force, although it is always tempting to do so. When the polish starts to dry, stop. Wait for it to dry, then rub it with dry, clean soft rags. You may need to do this several times. When the finish seems to shine and you can see reflections in it, it is ready for waxing.

Don't use brass polish on a factory-painted radio. If the finish is still in reasonable condition when all of the dirt is off, it is ready for waxing. A word of warning: Factory paint is almost impossible to strip. Don't try.

A good-quality hard car wax will give a good finish to either painted or unpainted plastic radios. A colored wax improves the sheen and color of Bakelite radios, but any good wax will help. It will take at least two or three coats; apply it sparingly and rub it out right away. If you apply a thick coat of wax to speed up the process, you will be disappointed. It takes enormous amounts of effort to polish a thick coat. You may even have to resort to turpentine to remove the wax buildup in order to start over. Stick with several light coats of wax. Once the radio looks good, it will gain a final sheen from a buffing with a lambskin buffer in a power drill.

11

Receiver Theory

This chapter details the operation of four types of receivers. The superheterodyne, being the most common, is covered first, even though it is the most complex. The tuned radio frequency and regenerative circuits used in older sets are examined as well. Finally we take a brief look at the crystal set. While this chapter is not essential for using the tips and guidelines in the rest of the book, it will help you understand the workings of circuit components. You may want to read other books on radio theory as well (see Chapter 12).

Superheterodyne Receivers

Fig. 11–1 shows a simplified block diagram of a common superheterodyne receiver. It will help you unravel the rather complicated ideas that follow.

A typical superheterodyne circuit from 1952 is shown in Figs. 11–2 and 11–3. Fig. 11–2 shows the chassis top arrangement and the standard circuit diagram. Fig. 11–3 shows placement of parts on the bottom of the chassis. These illustrations are of a Meissner 5 tube model 10-1191A but are similar to many sets of the era. We will look at it section by section. Read carefully and follow the circuit diagram as you go. It sometimes will help for you to draw a diagram of the section yourself.

Power Supply Section

In the power circuits, the filaments of the five tubes are connected in series across the power line. Notice that the filament voltages, expressed in the first tube number, are 12, 12, 12, 35, and 50, which add up to 121. Since this is close to the 115 volts the line supplies,

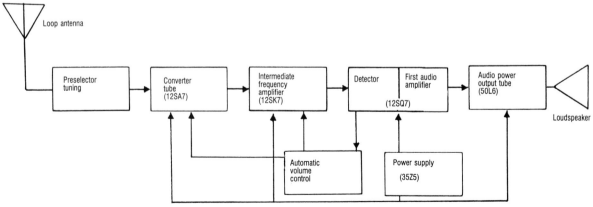

FIG. 11–1 *Superheterodyne radio block diagram.*

TUBE LAYOUT

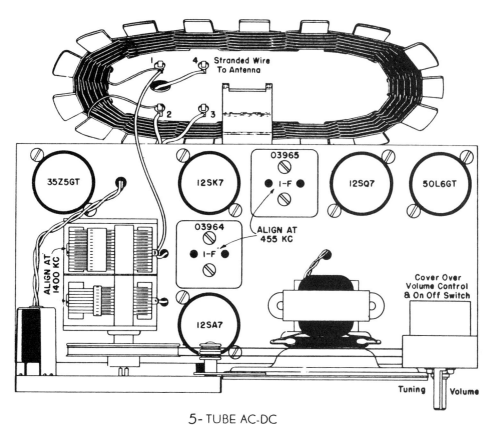

5- TUBE AC-DC
SCHEMATIC

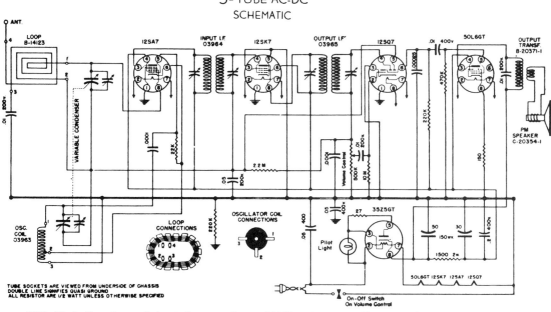

FIG. 11–2 *Top view and circuit diagram of typical 1950s AC-DC set (illustration from Meissner's " 'How to Build' Instruction Manual," Thordarson-Meissner, 1952).*

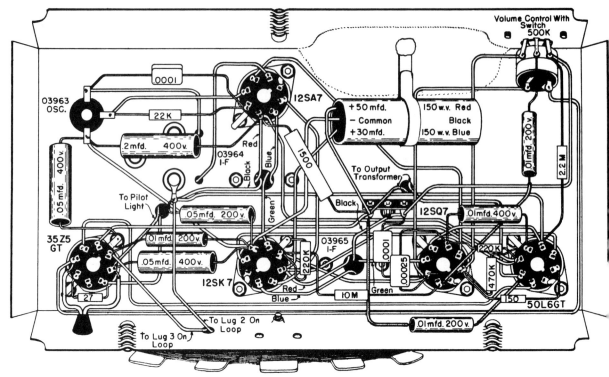

FIG. 11–3 *Underchassis view of five-tube AC-DC radio (illustration from Meissner's " 'How to Build' Instruction Manual," Thordarson-Meissner, 1952).*

the filaments can be series connected across the AC line without an extra resistance.

The B+ voltage is obtained from the 35Z5GT rectifier. AC is applied to the plate of the 35Z5GT through part of the 35Z5GT filament, the pilot light, and a 27-ohm resistor that gives surge protection. Rectified B+ is obtained from the cathode and is filtered by a 50-mfd. capacitor, a 1500-ohm 2-watt resistor, and a second capacitor, this time 30 mfd. This smooths the ripple in the DC. The .2 mfd. 400-volt paper capacitor acts to bypass any radio frequency signals to ground, making the radio more stable. A higher voltage for the audio output is taken off before the first filter capacitor. A slightly lower voltage for the other tubes comes off after the 1500-ohm filter resistor.

Preselector Tuning Section

In the antenna circuit, the loop antenna is also the antenna coil, and is tuned by half of the variable condenser to preselect the desired fre-

quency. The second variable condenser in parallel with the main section is a small mica trimmer condenser found on the side of the tuning condenser. It serves to adjust the loop for best reception at the top end of the dial. An extra loop of wire couples an outside antenna with the loop antenna through a .01 mfd. capacitor, avoiding a direct connection to the chassis ground while still allowing R.F. to flow through the loop.

Converter-Oscillator Section

In the converter circuit, the preselected signal from the loop arrives at grid 3 (pin 8) of the 12SA7 converter tube, where it is mixed with a signal generated in the same tube in the following way.

One end of the oscillator coil (terminal 1), is attached to the first grid (tube pin 5) through a .0001 mfd. capacitor (which keeps the DC bias on grid). The other end of the coil (terminal 3) goes to ground. Terminal 2 takes part of the signal to the cathode of the tube (tube pin

6). Any signal arriving at grid 1 is of such a phase in relation to the cathode that the tube will amplify its own signal and oscillate. Grids 2 and 4, which are internally connected, are fed B+ through tube pin 4 directly and are grounded, as far as any signal is concerned, through the filter condensers. Grid 2 acts as the plate for the oscillator section of the tube.

The oscillator is tuned to a frequency lower than that of the received frequency on grid 3 by the other half of the variable tuning condenser, which is in a tuned circuit with the oscillator coil. Since both halves of the tuning condenser have a single shaft, the oscillator will change frequency with the changing of the tuning condenser. The oscillator has its own trimmer adjustment to get exactly the right oscillator frequency difference.

The difference between the desired station and the lower oscillator frequency is called the intermediate frequency, or I.F. In modern AM superheterodyne receivers, the I.F. is usually about 455 kHz. In older superheterodynes it is often a lower frequency. Usually, the circuit diagram gives the I.F. frequency.

How do the two frequencies get mixed, and how do you get a new one? Remember that the cathode of the 12SA7 is supplying a current that varies in frequency with the oscillator. That same varying electron stream also is controlled by the preselected frequency signal on grid 3. The result is that on the plate of the 12SA7, there will be four frequencies. The oscillator frequency is (0), the preselected program frequency (P), and also P + 0 and P − 0.

The input I.F. transformer is tuned to P − 0, which is always the intermediate frequency. The other signals, being considerably different in frequency, are rejected.

The trimmer condensers on top of the input I.F. are used to tune its primary and secondary windings to the exact intermediate frequency. The 12SA7 receives its plate voltage and passes on this signal through the primary of the I.F. transformer.

One more point before we leave the converter: the 22k resistor between grid 1 and the cathode is necessary to provide a DC return to ground for grid 1, preventing electron build-up that would eventually block the grid. The resistance provides some bias to grid 1, which is kept on the grid by the .0001 mfd. blocking condenser. The necessary bias on grid 3 is obtained from the automatic volume control (AVC) circuit.

I.F. Amplifier Section

The 12SK7 is a pentode amplifier that amplifies the modulated I.F. signal. Grid 1 of the I.F. amplifier receives its signal from the secondary winding of the input I.F. transformer. The I.F. transformer has its signal circuit completed to ground through the .05 mfd. capacitor and its bias supplied by the AVC circuit through the same .05 mfd. capacitor and the 2.2 meg. resistor. The second or screen grid that makes high amplification in one tube possible receives its high voltage directly from B+. This grid greatly reduces the likelihood that the tube will oscillate by reducing its plate to grid capacity. The third, or suppressor, grid is attached directly to the grounded cathode. The suppressor drives back into the plate electrons knocked loose by the high electron stream velocity in this high-gain tube.

The plate of the 12SK7 receives its high voltage through the primary of the output I.F. transformer, which, like the input I.F., is tuned by trimmer condensers across its windings.

Detector Section

In the detector circuit, the I.F. signal, highly amplified across the secondary of the output I.F. transformer, is strong enough to act on the plate of one diode (pin 4) of the 12SQ7 tube. This diode becomes a rectifier, conducting when the plate end of the output I.F. is positive, allowing current then to flow through its secondary winding and through the volume control. The ground circuit for this receiver is indicated by the dark line on the circuit diagram.

The amount of current drawn will depend on how much the plate of the diode goes positive. Remember that the I.F. signal varies in amplitude (height or volume) with the original signal put on the carrier in the modulator at the transmitter (see Fig. 2–18).

Thus, the current through the volume control varies as the I.F. frequency of 455 kHz and the audio modulation. The .0001 capacitor across the volume control acts to take out the 455 kHz part of the signal, leaving the audio at the top of the volume control. A capacity of .0001 mfd. is too low to affect the audio portion of the signal.

Now that the original signal has been detected, only the original audio signal remains.

Automatic Volume Control Section

The automatic volume control (AVC) circuit begins at the other diode (12SQ7 pin 5), which connects to the bottom of the output I.F. transformer through a 2.2-meg resistor. The .05 mfd. 200-volt capacitor next to the 2.2-meg resistor acts to store a DC charge that varies slowly with the overall loudness of the signal. A DC charge will collect on one plate of the .05 capacitor, which slowly drains out through the 2.2-megohm resistor and the 500,000-ohm volume control.

By selecting resistance size and capacitor value carefully, we can have a negative charge that closely follows the power or loudness of the signal coming through the receiver. This negative voltage then changes with the power of the station. A weak station will generate only a small negative voltage at the .05 capacitor, and a loud local station will generate a large negative voltage.

Notice that the grids of the 12SA7 and the 12SK7 are connected at the same point. Those grids are all made more negative, and therefore, the amplification of those tubes decreased, by a loud station's signal. In effect, the loud station has its volume reduced, while the weak station does not have its volume decreased as much. The circuit acts as an AVC on the loud stations.

The actual loudness in the speaker is, of course, controlled by the volume control.

Audio Amplification Section

Since the cathode of the 12SQ7 is grounded in the first audio amplifier circuit, the grid of the triode section must obtain its negative bias through the 10-meg grid-leak resistor. A grid leak works this way: The grid of a tube, being in the electron stream from the cathode to the plate, collects some electrons each time it becomes more positive. As the electrons accumulate, they make the grid more negative. Eventually the grid will become sufficiently negative to block the flow of electrons from cathode to plate completely. The grid-leak resistance lets the surplus electrons leak at a rate slow enough to keep the grid at the desired slightly negative potential or voltage.

The audio signal exists across the volume control and is taped off by the slider of the control. The closer to the top the slider is, the louder the output. The .01 capacitor from the slider passes the audio signal to the grid of the 12SQ7 while holding the bias on the grid, so that the tube operates most efficiently.

The output of the amplifier is developed across the plate-load resistor (220k ohms) connected to pin 6 of the 12SQ7. As a varying current is drawn by the plate of the 12SQ7, there is a varying voltage drop across the resistor that is applied to the grid of the 50L6GT output tube. The .00025 mfd. capacitor filters out any remaining I.F. signal. The .01-mfd. capacitor from 12SQ7 pin 6 to the 50L6GT pin 5 acts to keep the high voltage from the plate of the 12SQ7 off the grid of the output tube.

In the power output circuit, the signal from the first audio tube is applied to the control grid of the 50L6GT power output tube. This grid is given a ground return through the 470k grid resistor. This resistance is not high enough in resistance to give the tube much negative grid bias, so bias for the tube is obtained by placing a 150-ohm resistor in the cathode circuit (pin 8). Current flowing through the tube causes the cathode to become slightly positive, which is the same thing as making the grid negative by an equal amount.

The second or screen grid is attached to B+ directly. The beam forming plates in this beam power tube serve much the same function as the suppressor grid in a pentode and are connected to the cathode. The plate of the 50L6GT receives its B+ through the primary winding of the output transformer, developing its signal in that primary. The .01 mfd. capacitor across the output transformer primary is called the tone condenser. It softens the tone by removing the higher A.F.s. It also helps remove background noise.

The output transformer transfers the audio signal energy to the lightweight, low-impedance voice coil of the permanent magnet (p.m.) speaker. When the varying current flows through this coil, it reacts with the magnetic field in the loudspeaker, moving the cone of the speaker and producing sound.

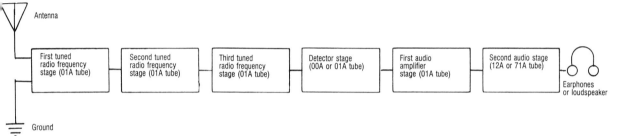

FIG. 11–4 *Functional block diagram of typical T.R.F. receiver.*

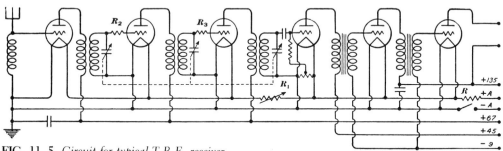

FIG. 11–5 *Circuit for typical T.R.F. receiver.*

Tuned Radio Frequency Receivers

Figs. 11–4 and 11–5 show a typical tuned radio frequency (T.R.F.) receiver from the mid-1920s. This was the design used by many classical-era receivers. The circuit is straightforward and simple. It can be powered by batteries or a power pack. Notice that it uses a considerable number of tubes, since all are low-amplification triodes.

You can see from the block diagram that the first three tubes are R.F. amplifiers, the fourth is the detector, and the last two are audio amplifiers. In most receivers of the era, all of the tubes except the last audio amplifier are '01As.

In the power circuits, the filaments of the tubes are all fed from a 6-volt source (the A voltage), usually from an auto-type storage battery. The tubes used have 5-volt filaments. There is a fixed series resistor (R) that drops the voltage to the audio tubes and the detector. The R.F. tube filaments are also controlled by a rheostat (R1). This will affect the sensitivity of the receiver (the ability to receive distant stations). This receiver has another control to adjust the bias on the detector, also controlling the volume of the set. Other T.R.F. receivers sometimes do the same thing by putting a separate rheostat in the detector filament circuit.

The B voltage must be supplied at three different voltage levels. The three R.F. tubes and the first audio tube require $67\frac{1}{2}$ volts. The output tube needs a higher voltage that depends on the type of tube used. The detector of this set requires 45 volts. Other designs need only $22\frac{1}{2}$ volts. The $67\frac{1}{2}$ volt line is bypassed to ground through a fixed paper condenser, which helps to prevent oscillation.

The antenna circuit usually requires an outside antenna and a good ground.

The tuning condensers in this and other R.F. sections may be fastened together with belts or be on the same shaft so that all are tuned at once. In other sets each may be tuned separately, a difficult job at best.

The first R.F. amplifier is not tuned, but the other R.F. amplifier stages are identical. In each grid circuit, the secondary winding of the R.F. transformer, being tuned to resonate with the desired frequency, will reduce other frequencies giving stronger amplification of the desired station. This selection will increase in each stage. There is a small fixed resistor (R2 and R3) in each grid circuit to aid stability.

A small amount of grid bias is obtained by

RECEIVER THEORY

Heathkit model W-4B hi-fi amplifier. Although somewhat less expensive than other Heathkit models, it still is a good-quality amplifier kit.

Heathkit circa 1957–1958 model W-5M twenty-watt amplifier in gold color painted metal. This is a very high quality tube-type amplifier.

Heathkit 1960 model SP 2A stereo preamplifier. The interesting design integrates two separate monaural preamplifiers, which allows for very flexible switching.

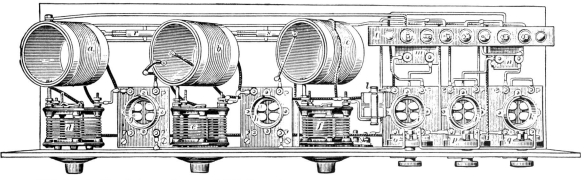

FIG. 11–6 *Chassis layout for typical T.R.F. receiver.*

having the filament go positive from B−, which is also ground. This is done by connecting B− and A− together. The grid will see this as if it were a negative potential on the grid.

The plate of each tube is coupled through the primary of an R.F. transformer to the next stage, receiving its B+ through the primary.

Detection is aided in this triode tube in two ways. First, there is a comparatively large negative grid bias on the tube because of a high-resistance grid leak. The grid condenser in the grid circuit keeps the bias on the grid, so that it does not leak off through the transformer. The bias can be adjusted using the control across the detector filament, reducing it, by making that point more positive. A high negative bias encourages plate current cutoff on negative swings of the grid.

The other factor encouraging rectification is the low plate voltage (45 volts) that operates the tube near the bottom of its conducting range, again keeping it from conducting if the grid is very negative.

Thus, the signal passes and is amplified only when it is positive enough to overcome the grid bias and the low plate voltage. Some receivers use a phone condenser, a small-capacity mica capacitor, from the detector plate to its filament. This filters out the R.F. portion of the rectified output, leaving only the audio. The set pictured in Fig. 11–5 does not use one.

The first audio tube works exactly as the R.F. amplifier tubes do, with one exception: the coupling between stages is done using iron core transformers, which are more efficient than air core transformers at audio frequencies.

Generally, the tube used in the output tube circuit is designed to carry more current and thus supply the greater power needed to operate the listening device. It differs from the first audio amplifier in a few ways: First, it uses C battery bias (in this case −9 volts) to set firmly the negative grid bias in order to give the most undistorted output for the tube type chosen. In most classic battery receivers, the power or output tube is coupled directly to the listening device. The plate current of the output tube flows through the earphones or magnetic speaker. Since the current varies with the A.F. signal, the variations produce sound.

Fig. 11–6 is an overhead view of another typical T.R.F. receiver of this area. It gives a good idea of how the chassis is laid out. This particular set shows sockets for two R.F. amplifier tubes.

Regenerative Receivers

A simple receiver system, commonly used in early one-tube sets and later as a detector in some T.R.F. receivers, is called the regenerative detector. It is an oscillator tube arrangement that is not quite allowed to oscillate.

Examine Fig. 11–7 to see how it works. The antenna picks up a mixture of R.F. signals, causing a small current to flow in the primary winding of coil L-1 to ground. This current is stepped up in voltage in the secondary winding, which has more turns of wire. The secondary winding of L-1 is tuned to resonate at the

RECEIVER THEORY

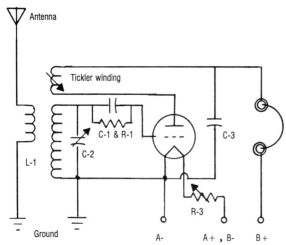

FIG. 11–7 *Typical one-tube regenerative receiver.*

frequency desired by tuning condenser C-2. This acts to select the desired station. This selected signal is sent to the grid of the triode tube through condenser C-1. The tube then amplifies the signal selected. As electrons flow from filament to plate in the tube, some collect on the grid. They leak off through the high resistance, R-1, but a rather high negative bias remains on the grid.

The tube, much like the T.R.F. detector, only amplifies the positive part of the signal on the grid, acting as a rectifier. In order to increase amplification and sensitivity, part of the amplified signal on the plate is fed back into the grid by means of tickler winding on L-1. It is fed back in such a way as to increase the signal on the grid, forcing the tube to amplify itself.

If too much signal is fed back, the tube becomes an oscillator and all signal is lost. If the right amount is fed back, the tube becomes a very powerful amplifier. The tickler winding is made movable so the coupling can be varied for the right amount of feedback. Once the

signal is amplified, it is smoothed by C-3, with the high-frequency R.F. being removed. The signal current to the plate flows across the resistance of the headphones, which turn that varying current supplied by the B battery into sound.

Overall volume of the receiver is controlled by the filament rheostat, R-3.

A simpler triode tube-type detector can be made by not using the tickler winding. This becomes the simple grid leak detector, which usually needs outside amplification to be effective.

Crystal Receivers

The most simple design of all is the crystal detector receiver. Fig. 11–8 shows both the circuit and a pictorial of the wiring of a Crystal set. Crystal sets can use only the actual power of the radio waves in the air to produce sound, so they must be close to the station to work.

A long antenna (c) is wired through the primary (a) of the input transformer to a good

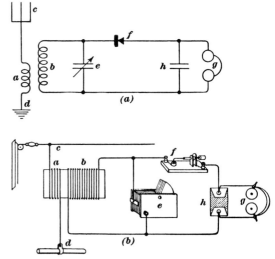

FIG. 11–8 *Circuit diagram (A) and wiring layout (B) for crystal radio.*

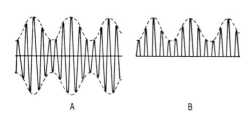

A   B   C

FIG. 11–9 *Waveforms found in crystal radios.*

General Electric 1946 model 220 five-tube AC/DC brown Bakelite radio.

Emerson 1947 model 540A brown Bakelite five-tube AC/DC radio. This was one of the smallest five-tube AC/DC sets ever built, and measures $6\frac{3}{8} \times 4\frac{7}{8} \times 4\frac{1}{2}$ inches. The knobs are not original.

Arvin 1955 model 954P green four-tube plus selenium rectifier three-way portable radio.

ground (d). The voltage increases somewhat because the secondary coil of the input transformer (b) has more turns of wire. The secondary winding (b) is tuned by a variable condenser (e) to select the station desired. Fig. 11–9, example A shows a typical modulated R.F. signal.

The crystal (f) acts as a one-way valve (it works like a tube diode) and only conducts electricity in one direction. The electric current coming out of the detector will be a rapidly varying direct current with variations of the frequency of the broadcast station and of the audible frequency placed on that carrier frequency at the station. Fig. 11–9, example B shows how it looks. The phone condenser (h) filters out that R.F. carrier, leaving only the varying audible signal to be heard in the earphones (g). This corresponds to Fig. 11–9, example C.

12
Your Electronics Shop

If you are restoring only one or two radios, you will not need much more than a card table, good lighting, a few basic tools, and a cigar box for parts. You will be working slowly but will get the job done. Even starting small, you will need some things. This chapter gives a few tips about ordering. Except for purchasing basic tools and test equipment, two rules are important: Don't buy anything expensive until you need it, and watch for used equipment at flea markets and antique malls. You may have to do some clean-up and repair, but you'll save a pile of money and get some excellent equipment too.

Basic Tools

Most of the items listed below are available at a good hardware, Radio Shack, or old radio supply store.

- Soldering gun (at least 100 watts). These are far more useful than the little soldering irons or soldering pencils used for printed circuit boards.
- High-quality long-nose pliers
- Good-quality diagonal wire cutters
- Small Phillips and regular screwdrivers
- Nut driver set
- Utility knife
- Pair of tweezers
- Set of plastic alignment tools
- Soldering aids (These look like dentist's tools and are useful for prying, twisting, and poking things into place. Buy both the split-end and bent-end types.)

- Insulated test wires (at least four) with clips at both ends

Buying the best tools that Radio Shack sells, the above list will cost you about $50 in 1992 prices. You probably have some of the tools already. You may also find some better prices or sales.

Useful Tools

Here is a list of other useful tools. These are less necessary but might still be helpful.

- Regular pliers
- 1" soft paint brush
- Hex wrench set
- Wire stripper
- Forceps, for holding wires in place and for draining off heat while soldering in parts
- Set of open-end and box wrenches
- Work light on flexible arm
- Small compressor
- Small vacuum cleaner
- Tool box

The compressor is very useful for cleaning out chassis (and pumping up auto tires and beach balls). It is an amazingly useful general tool around the house.

Test Equipment

These suggestions are listed in order of importance. No beginner would want or could afford all of these, but some are essential. When you buy a piece of test equipment, read the accompanying instructions carefully and keep them. Buy books on the use of the equipment you acquire if possible.

Equipment marked with three bullets is essential. Two-bullet items are very useful to persons doing much service or restoring. One-bullet items are nice to have but not necessary. The ○-marked items are specialized; you might want them sometime.

● ● ● **Multitester.** This volt-ohm milli-ammeter is your single most useful electrical tool. Multitesters are available from many sources. An adequate unit costs from $20 to $50. See Fig. 12–1 for an example of one service-type multitester. Your tester should have at least 10,000 ohms-per-volt sensitivity on the DC voltage scale. It should be capable of measuring resistances of up to 1 megohm accurately. The meter type of tester is fine for your work. The newer digital units cost more and are more accurate, but not that much more helpful. I use both types.

Radio Shack stores sell a wide variety of multitesters. They also sell a good book entitled *Using Your Meter*, which will help you a great deal in using your tester and doing any electrical testing.

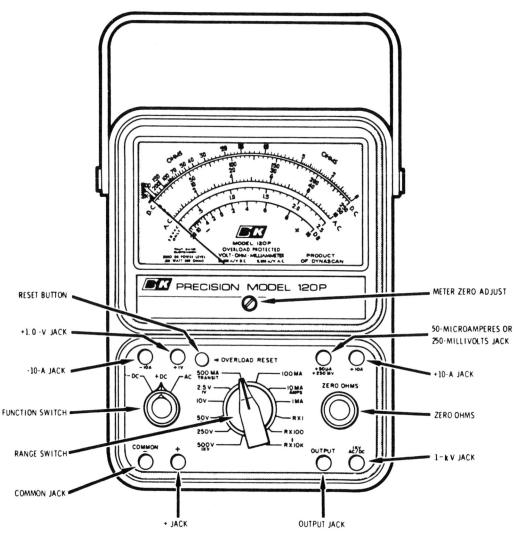

FIG. 12–1 *Typical high-grade multitester. Courtesy B&K Division of Dynascan Corporation.*

A high-quality 1948 service oscilloscope by Hickok, as shown in Radio News, *October 1948.*

Most of the time, look for good used equipment. In the case of a multitester, buy a new one. Used ones are often damaged and the test prods worn out. Since new ones are readily available, there is no reason not to buy new. The exception here might be if you find a good vacuum tube voltmeter. These are often around, and if you find one with a good test probe, you will find it accurate and useful.

● ● ● **Ground fault interrupter.** This little device looks like a regular 120-volt outlet but is designed to detect any electrical currents to ground that are not normal and to shut off the electrical power if such a ground leak is found. That ground leak could go through your body and kill you. My shop is located in a damp basement, so the whole electronics shop is run through ground fault interrupter, a (GFI). This is essential protection.

If you use older test equipment, you may find that your GFI switches off frequently for no known reason. This is because the line filter capacitors in your piece of equipment, from the 120-volt line to ground, have started to leak, which means too much electrical current is flowing through them. This may be enough to cause the GFI to "trip," or shut off. The only way to solve the problem is to replace the capacitors with new ones of the same capacity and a 600-volt or more voltage rating.

It is easy to turn on the GFI again. There is a small reset button on the front of the unit. See Chapter 5 again for more information on the GFI.

● ● ● **Isolation transformer.** This device protects you from the 120-volt line and may in some models give you a way to vary its output voltage in testing your radio. It will allow you to increase the line voltage fed to an AC set gradually, which can help you find power supply problems before they cause damage. It will allow you to run an intermittent radio at a high line voltage to force it to act up. But most importantly, it will completely protect you from line shock hazard on an AC/DC set.

Isolation transformers are available in many forms, some very expensive. Several are available from Antique Electronics Supply. Other professional-quality units can be obtained from Fordham Radio. See the end of this chapter for plans for building a unit with parts from Radio Shack that will work for smaller AC/DC sets.

● ● **Signal injector.** This instrument produces a broad band electrical signal that can be used to test both R.F. and A.F. amplifier stages. It is not particularly useful in tuning or aligning a set. You don't need one if you plan to use the more useful R.F. signal generator. Injectors are available at low cost from Antique Electronics Supply, which calls it a circuit tester.

● ● **R.F. signal generator.** A signal generator, which will produce modulated signals of any frequency needed, is almost essential for any alignment of radios and is very helpful in troubleshooting. Try to find a unit that will produce signals from 100 kHz. to at least 20 mHz. These are available from any radio service supply source.

Good basic units are available new in the $150 price range from several sources. Fordham Electric has several. You can also find many used ones on the market. Look for Heathkit and Eico models; they are simple and reliable. You can find them for less than $50 if you look. I use a Heathkit IG-102, one of their cheapest models, which does the job well. Two other nice ones are the Eico 324 and 330.

Here's a tip: If you get a used generator it is probably out of alignment; that is, the frequency on the dial will be 5 to 10 percent off from the actual frequency produced. Try to avail yourself of a frequency counter to reset your generator. The instruction book for the generator will tell you where the adjustment points are in your unit. If you have no instructions, simply make a chart that shows what the dial of your generator must be set for to produce several accurate frequencies. You want to be able to get accurate frequencies of 455 kHz, 600 kHz, 1000 kHz, 1500 kHz, 5 mHz, 10 mHz, 10.7 mHz, and 20 mHz. Knowing the dial setting on your generator for those, you can find almost any frequency you need with enough accuracy to do your work.

The best thing to do is buy a frequency counter (Fordham Electric again) and attach it permanently to the signal generator. This makes finding the frequency desired very easy. It is useful for aligning signal generators as well. Some of the more expensive signal generators made now have the frequency counter built in.

● ● **Tube tester.** No one manufactures a tester today that will test the four-, five-, six-, and seven-pin tubes found in older sets. Used tube testers that will do this can be found at older radio-television repair shops. Many radio amateurs or hobbyists will have one. Check the ads in newsletters that serve antique radio collectors, or watch for them in antiques malls or flea markets. They will cost anywhere from $5 to $100. The one I use most cost me $5.

● ● **Test loudspeaker.** You can make a test loudspeaker from an old permanent magnet (p.m.) speaker in a cabinet and an output transformer from an old radio. Make sure you are able to use the speaker with or without the output transformer. See the end of this chapter for a suggested circuit of one you can build easily. If you are going to test an output tube directly, you will need the output transformer. The speaker can be used directly to replace a p.m. or a dynamic speaker. If you use it to test a field coil speaker, leave the field coil on the original speaker connected to the set. Even better, find a used signal tracer unit such as an Eico 145. This is a test speaker and transformer with extra features, such as a built-in amplifier. Again, if you look you can find them available.

● ● **Series light tester.** This is not necessary if you plan to buy or build an adjustable voltage isolation transformer. You can build a series light tester by mounting two ordinary surface switch boxes and a surface mount light box on a suitably sized board. Fig. 12–2 shows a series tester with a switch. Wire from your 120-volt line cord through switch (1), in series with a light socket (3), and to an ordinary double outlet (2).

By screwing a high-wattage (200 watts or so) light bulb into the light socket, you can make a unit that will protect anything plugged into it from electrical overload and still allow the radio plugged into the tester to run at nearly normal voltage. The higher the wattage bulb used, the higher the output voltage will be at the double outlet. By using different-sized bulbs, you can send a reduced voltage to any radio you want to run at low voltage.

● ● **Condenser tester.** This is a very useful unit that does two things: First, it measures (not very accurately) the capacity of a condenser (now called capacitors). Most condensers have their capacity marked on them. The tester will show if a condenser is open or has lost capacity for any reason. Some restorers simply replace all condensers.

I find that the greatest value of a condenser tester is to test for leakage. Most old radio condensers are likely to leak (that is, pass DC in when they should not). A large share of radio problems are caused by these leaky condensers. A condenser tester will find these. If you have a leaking condenser, replace it.

Any time you make a capacity or voltage measurement on a condenser, make sure at least one wire is completely disconnected from the circuit to which it was connected.

To my knowledge, no one manufactures a condenser tester that will test for leakage at high voltages, so you will have to look for a used one. I use an Eico 950. Most of the service-type condenser testers are similar.

● **Power supply.** When you are testing or using a classic-era battery set, farm radio, or newer tube-type battery radio, you will need a power supply. These used to be called battery eliminators. This will provide a variety of voltages needed to use or test old radios. Several individuals make these for sale, and they are not very difficult to design or build. If you look through any of the antique radio collector's magazines, you in time will find a circuit you can use. If you want to, you can obtain a kit or several different ready-built units from Antique Electronics Supply .

● **Line voltage meter.** This handy but unnecessary item is not a service instrument but a little meter you leave plugged into the AC line. On an expanded scale (from 100 to 140 volts), it shows how much voltage you are using. If you are in a brownout it can be helpful to know just what is happening. Fordham Electric has two: one currently available for $100 and one for $25.

● **Oscilloscope.** This television-like instrument allows you to see the nature of the waveform of any electrical signal in a set. It is useful for signal tracing, finding distortion, spotting high-frequency oscillations, and so forth but is not essential for the beginner. It is expensive. If you buy a new one, get a triggered sweep type. A new unit for the serious hobbyist will cost from $250 to $500. Professional electronics service personnel use these scopes a great deal. I have a nice old Tektronics 535 dating from the 1960s that originally cost several thousand dollars. It is a real electric heater (about 70 tubes) and works beautifully.

If you don't want one that complicated, you can sometimes find other used oscilloscopes in the $50-to-$100 range. These can be unreliable, so don't buy one used without having a chance to test it to see if it will sync various frequency signals and has a green trace that doesn't drift off the screen after a few minutes. It takes a while to learn to use the scope, but professionals find it invaluable.

○ **Audio generator.** If you are going to service hi-fi equipment or use an oscilloscope for audio testing, you may want a good audio

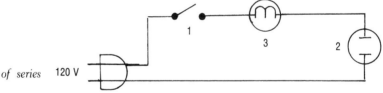

FIG. 12–2 *Diagram of series light tester.*

Zenith 1950 model 516Y chassis 5G03 five-tube AC/DC clock radio in black Bakelite with gold bezel.

Crosley 1946 model 66TA brown Bakelite six-tube AC AM/SW radio. Model 66TW featured white-painted Bakelite; 66TC was made of wood.

Zenith 1948 AM/FM chassis 7E01 brown Bakelite seven-tube and selenium rectifier AC/DC AM/FM radio.

generator. Again, used ones are in the $20-to-$50 range. The Eico 379 or Heathkit IG-48 are good service models. These produce sine and square waves. Square waves are particularly useful with an oscilloscope for amplifier testing. Modern function generators can also be used as audio oscillators and can often be found quite cheaply.

○ **Distortion analyzer.** We are getting into very expensive hardware here. Don't worry about them unless you will be servicing tube-type hi-fi equipment. They are hard to find, and new ones cost more than $1000. I found a used Heathkit IM-5258 that's nice to have but isn't used much.

○ **FM generator.** This is not necessary for most work but is nice for aligning FM stereo receivers. A Heathkit IG-37 is useful if you can find one.

Since I enjoy collecting and working with old test equipment, I have a whole shop full of it. Very few restorers would want this much stuff. The old test gear can be interesting and often works very well. In many cases it is the only equipment available, since it is no longer manufactured.

Beware: When you buy used test equipment, it may need some repair. Try to get operating instructions. Most old test equipment is fairly simple and has many of the same faults as radios from the same era. Because it is sometimes hard for the beginner to work on, try to buy used equipment with the right to return it if it doesn't work properly.

Shop Supplies

Some supplies are very helpful to have. They don't cost much, so even if you are just starting out, keep them on hand.

- Solder (60 percent tin, 40 percent lead rosin core)
- Desoldering braid (useful for cleaning solder from a connection you wish to take apart)
- Television tuner-cleaner spray
- Black electrical tape
- Pack of colored tapes (useful for marking wires and connections)
- WD-40 lubricant spray
- Dry powdered rosin (available from music stores)

- Contact cement (which remains flexible)
- Household cement

Useful Substitute Testing or Replacement Parts

It is good, even for the beginner, to have a few new parts on hand for repair and substitution. The bare minimum is noted in the list that follows. You don't need to stock many, since they are available from a number of sources, like Antique Electronics Supply. If you work with old radios, you will want to develop a source for replacement parts.

I keep parts sets of different kinds on hand. These are old radios with ruined cabinets or that are damaged in some way so that they are not fixable. These can be a cheap and valuable source of parts and tubes that you will need. You often can find them for next to nothing at junk shops. Remember to test carefully the parts you remove to make sure they are good before installing them in a radio.

Here is my list of what I would stock new. The total cost of this list is under $10.

- 22 mfd. 450-volt electrolytic capacitor
- .1 mfd. 600-volt capacitor
- .01 mfd. 600-volt capacitor
- 100-ohm 10-watt resistor
- 500,000-ohm volume control
- 470,000-ohm $\frac{1}{2}$-watt carbon resistor
- 100,000-ohm $\frac{1}{2}$-watt carbon resistor
- 10,000-ohm $\frac{1}{2}$-watt carbon resistor
- 2,200-ohm $\frac{1}{2}$-watt carbon resistor
- 470-ohm $\frac{1}{2}$-watt carbon resistor
- #47 pilot light

Don't stock any tubes until you see what types of radios you are working on. If you have a tube tester, check the pull-outs—tubes you have taken from unrepairable radios. Most of the tubes will be usable if you can test them. Some repairers use this rule: when you need a tube, order two. The extra one goes into stock. Tubes are readily available from many sources, Antique Electronics Supply being one.

Shop Tips

Removing parts (desoldering connections). Heat the joint you wish to disconnect carefully

The specs prove it...your best buy is EICO ®

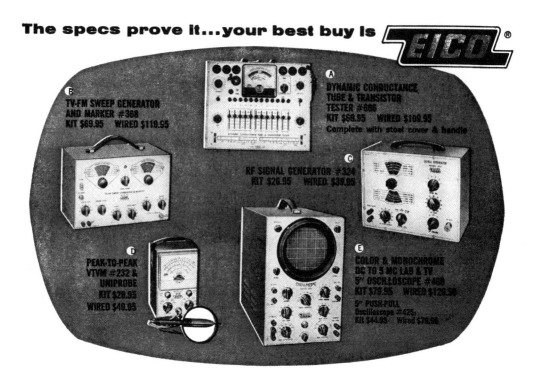

A DYNAMIC CONDUCTANCE TUBE & TRANSISTOR TESTER #666 KIT $68.95 WIRED $109.95 Complete with steel cover & handle

B TV-FM SWEEP GENERATOR AND MARKER #368 KIT $69.95 WIRED $119.95

C RF SIGNAL GENERATOR #324 KIT $26.95 WIRED $39.95

D PEAK-TO-PEAK VTVM #232 & UNIPROBE KIT $29.95 WIRED $49.95

E COLOR & MONOCHROME DC TO 5 MC LAB & TV 5" OSCILLOSCOPE #460 KIT $79.95 WIRED $129.50

5" PUSH-PULL Oscilloscope #425; Kit $44.95 Wired $79.95

● Tests all receiving tubes (picture tubes with adapter), n-p-n and p-n-p transistors. Composite indication of Gm, Gp & peak emission. Simultaneous selection of any one of 4 combinations of 3 plate voltages, 3 screen voltages, 3 ranges of continuously variable grid voltage (with 5% accurate pot.). Sensitive 200 ua meter. 10 six-position lever switches: freepoint connection of each tube pin. 10 pushbuttons: rapid insert of any tube element in leakage test circuit. Direct reading of inter-element leakage in ohms. New gear-driven rollchart. **CRA Adapter $4.50.**

● Entirely electronic sweep circuit with accurately-biased increductor for excellent linearity. Extremely flat RF output. Exceptional tuning accuracy. Hum and leakage eliminated. 5 fund. sweep ranges: 3-216 mc. Variable marker range: 2-75 mc

in 3 fund. bands, 60-225 mc on harmonic band. 4.5 xtal marker osc., xtal supplied. Ext. marker provision. Attenuators: Marker Size, RF Fine, RF Coarse (4-step decade). Narrow range phasing control for accurate alignment.

● 150 kc to 435 mc with ONE generator in 6 fund. bands and 1 harmonic band! ±1.5% freq. accuracy. Colpitts RF osc. directly plate-modulated by K-follower for improved mod. Variable depth of int. mod. 0-50% by 400 cps Colpitts osc. Variable gain ext. mod. amplifier: only 3.0 v needed for 30% mod. Turret-mounted, slug-tuned coils for max. accuracy. Fine and Coarse (3-step) RF attenuators. RF output 100,000 uv, AF output to 10 v.

● Uni-Probe — exclusive with EICO — only 1 probe performs all functions: half-turn of probe tip selects DC or AC-Ohms. Calibration without re-

moving from cabinet. Measure directly p-p voltage of complex & sine waves: 0-4, 14, 42, 140, 420, 1400, 4200. DC/RMS sine volts: 0-1.5, 5, 15, 50, 150, 500, 1500 (up to 30,000 v. with HVP probe, & 250 mc with PRF probe). Ohms: 0.2 ohms to 1000 megs. 4½" meter, can't-burn-out circuit. 7 non-skip ranges on every function. Zero center.

● Features DC amplifiers! Flat from DC to 4.5 mc, usable to 10 mc. Vert. Sens.: 25 mv/in.; input Z 3. megs; direct-coupled & push-pull throughout. 4-step freq.-compensated attenuator up to 1000:1. Sweep: perfectly linear 10 cps — 100 kc (ext. cap. for range to 1 cps). Preset TV V & H positions. Auto sync. lim. & ampl. Direct or cap. coupling; bal. or unbal. inputs; edge-lit engraved lucite screen with dimmer control; plus many more outstanding features.

FREE CATALOG shows you HOW TO SAVE 50% on 65 models of top quality professional test equipment. MAIL COUPON NOW!

New Transistor Portable Radio RA-6 Kit $29.95 Wired $49.95 Incl. F.E.T.; less 9V batt Prealigned RF, IF xfmrs; push-pull audio; 6" spkr.

NEW Power & Bias Supply for Transistorized Eqpt. #1020 Kit $19.95 Wired $27.95

NEW Tube & CRT Fil. Tester #612 Kit $3.95 Wired $5.95 Fast-checks radio/TV tubes, pilot lamps, etc.

Series/Parallel R-C Combination Box #1140 Kit $13.95 Wired $19.95

Tube Tester #625 Kit $34.95 Wired $49.95 ● tests 600 mil series string type tubes ● illuminated roll-chart **Pix Tube Test Adapter** $4.50

6V & 12V Battery Eliminator & Charger #1050 Kit $29.95 Wired $38.95 Extra-filtered for transistor equipt. **#1060** Kit $38.95 Wired $47.95

20,000 Ohms/Volt V-O-M #565 Kit $24.95 Wired $29.95 **1000 Ohms/Volt V-O-M #536** Kit $12.90 Wired $14.90

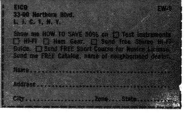

EICO ®

33-00 Northern Blvd. L.I.C. 1, N.Y.

Add 5% in the West.

TURN PAGE FOR MORE EICO VALUES

R-C Bridge & R-C-L Comparator #950B Kit $19.95 Wired $29.95 Reads 0.5 ohms-500 megs; 10 mmfd-5000 mfd, power factor

VTVM Probes

	Kit	Wired
Peak-to-Peak	$4.95	$6.95
RF	$3.75	$4.95
High Voltage Probe-1		$6.95
High Voltage Probe-2		$4.95

Scope Probes

Demodulator	$3.75	$5.75
Direct	$2.75	$3.95
Low Capacity	$3.75	$5.75

EICO   EW-9
33-00 Northern Blvd.
L. I. C. 1, N. Y.

Show me HOW TO SAVE 50% on ☐ Test Instruments ☐ HI-FI ☐ Ham Gear. ☐ Send free Stereo Hi-Fi Guide. ☐ Send FREE Short Course for Novice License. Send me FREE Catalog, name of neighborhood dealer.

Name..................................

Address................................

City...............Zone.....State......

Eico made a line of service instrument and hi-fi kits as extensive as Heath's line. They were simple, reliable, and well-designed instruments. This ad is from Electronics World, *September 1960.*

with a soldering iron. As the solder starts to melt, use desoldering braid to soak up the melted solder. After it cools, cut off the soaked end of braid. Bare copper braid must always touch the joint. When you have removed as much solder as you can in this way, use the soldering tool with the double end to work the wire loose. You may be able to cut away parts of the wire to get it loose. Remove bits that you cut from the chassis.

Sometimes the job can be made easier by cutting away the part to be removed, leaving about $\frac{1}{8}$ inch at the joint. It may be easier to work the wire end out. Other times, if you are disposing of the part, it may be as easy to cut it away, leaving about $\frac{1}{2}$ inch of wire. This then can be twisted around the wire from the new part and the wires soldered.

Beware: Do not splash solder around the chassis or tube socket. Solder splashes can cause short circuits. Carefully remove any spills. A pair of tweezers is helpful here.

Soldering. The surfaces to be soldered must be clean. Use steel wool a distance away from the chassis to clean parts. Never use steel wool near or in the chassis. Bits of steel from the pad can cause serious problems, such as short-circuiting components or getting picked up by the loudspeaker magnet.

When making a connection to a terminal or another wire, make a mechanical bond by hooking in the wire. Touch the joint with the iron and heat it for a few seconds. Touch solder to the point where the iron touches the joint. Melt on just enough solder to cover the joint. Remove the iron and cool the joint with pliers.

Do not heat the joint longer than necessary to flow on the solder smoothly. Excessive and prolonged heat sometimes will damage condensers and resistors. If not enough heat is used, the joint will have insufficient solder flow. This joint will develop a high resistance later and give trouble. Solder should flow over the entire joint with the wire.

Burns. You probably will get small burns on your hands from your soldering iron or solder splashes. If you do, immediately run cold water over the burn, even if it doesn't hurt. Every time it starts to hurt, cool it again with water. Cover it only if it has blistered or if the skin is broken. See Chapter 5 for more information.

Electrical shock danger. Do not work on electrical equipment in an environment where you are grounded; that is, where any part of your body or work surface can contact the ground. This is important! If you come into contact with any voltage in relation to that ground, you become a resistor, and an electric current will flow through you. It takes only about $\frac{1}{100}$ of an ampere to kill under the right circumstances. If you haven't done so, read Chapter 5 for a detailed discussion of the dangers. Remember that there are high voltages in any working radio chassis. Make all repairs, and as many tests as you can, with the power off and the chassis unplugged from the 120-volt line.

Working with old electronic equipment is not particularly dangerous if you are careful. Knowledge of electricity and deliberate caution give you the protection you need. When in doubt, check with your voltmeter.

Equipment you can build. In addition to the series light tester described earlier in this chapter, there are two other useful pieces of equipment that you can put together.

Test speaker. This is useful as a quick replacement speaker for testing radios and for providing a built-in output transformer for further testing of a questionable output transformer. See Fig. 12–3 for a diagram of one I built. Most of the parts can come from a junked radio. You will need a five-to-eight-inch permanent magnet (P.M.) speaker (skr on the diagram). This can be old, but it should be in good condition. You will need to make some sort of cabinet for the speaker. You will need an output transformer (T1 on the diagram). This can come from any old radio with a single output tube. You will need S1, a single pole switch (SPDT), and R1, a 1-watt resistor that can be anything from 10 to 50 ohms. You will also need four banana plug

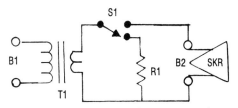

FIG. 12–3 *Test speaker with output transformer.*

binding posts for making connections in and out of the speaker. These pairs of binding posts are marked B1 and B2 on the diagram.

To use the unit, S1 is switched to the R1 side, and the clip leads that go to the speaker connections in the radio are connected to binding posts B2. You might mark this position on your switch speaker. Switched the other way, you can connect your test leads to B1 and the other ends to the plate of the output tube in your radio and to B+. You might mark that position on the switch transformer. The purpose of S1 is to remove T1 from the circuit when you are using the speaker alone.

Isolation transformer. Chapter 5 emphasized the importance of using an isolation transformer, particularly on AC/DC sets. See Fig. 12–4 for a unit that was built from parts obtained at a local Radio Shack store for about $40. It will provide a satisfactory and safe output to radios requiring up to about 60 watts.

For T1 and T2 in the diagram, any large filament-type transformer will do. Both should have the same secondary voltage. The transformers in this unit are 25.2-volt 2-amp transformers, the largest that Radio Shack sells. Higher-amp transformers would be better. Don't use transformers smaller than these 25-volt units.

You could simply wire the transformers' 25.2-volt winding to 25.2-volt winding, and put a plug on one 120-volt end and an outlet on the other 120-volt end and have a useful isolation transformer. This design adds a couple of useful features and puts it all in a cabinet. S3 is simply an on/off single-pole switch. Resistors R1 and R2 are 2-ohm and 5-ohm 10-watt units. S1 and S2 are single-pole switches handling 6 amps of current.

Stop and think about how they work. With both S1 and S2 turned on (closed), this acts as a simple isolation transformer with the two 25.2-volt windings connected together. If S1 is opened, you will have a 2-ohm resistor in series, slightly reducing the voltage arriving at the 25.2-volt winding of T2 and reducing the output voltage somewhat. If S2 is opened, you have 5 ohms in series, further reducing the output. If both S1 and S2 are opened, you will have 7 ohms in series, and the winding and the output will be yet lower. This means that if you want to bring up the operating voltage of your receiver slowly while you watch for problems, you can do it by opening and closing S1 and S2. You have an adjustable voltage isolation transformer. Locate R1 and R2; they will get hot when they are in the circuit, so make sure they do not touch wires and have some ventilation.

Here are a couple of other points: When I needed a line plug and wire and an output plug, I simply bought a short extension cord and cut it in two parts. I also added two insulated pin jacks across the output side of T2 in order to look at the output voltage with an AC voltmeter. This way, I know exactly what voltage is being fed to the radio.

When you build this or any other piece of equipment, plan ahead where you will put parts. Work neatly, and be careful that touching parts are properly insulated from each other.

Service Literature

Finding circuit diagrams and service instructions can be difficult. It is good to subscribe to an antique radio magazine and to belong to at least one club. Magazine ads give sources for diagrams. Watch for sales of old television shops, or for dealers specializing in old electronics in antiques malls or flea markets.

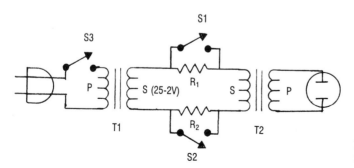

FIG. 12–4 *Circuit of isolation transformer.*

The manufacturer of this portable radio is unknown because the decal has worn away. Stylistically, this is typical of many small personal battery portables. It features a linen luggage-style case.

Heathkit circa 1950 model TC-1 tube tester.

1992 Micronta (Radio Shack) model 22-220 FET multitester. This is a good example of a modern test meter that also is useful for old radio work.

Homemade radio shop test speaker

Three main sources for service information were published in the days of tube-type radios. Two are out of business, although one has been reprinted to some extent.

Supreme *Most Often Used Radio Diagrams* were published each year from 1939 through the 1960s. There also was a useful diagram book covering 1926 through 1938. These include only a sampling of diagrams, but you often will find something close to the radio you are working on. Each volume is about $\frac{3}{4}$-inch thick. These will probably be the least expensive. I have seen some reprinted but don't know of a source.

Rider manuals. There are 23 of these loose-leaf volumes, varying in thickness from 3 inches to $5\frac{1}{2}$ inches thick. These include other service data in addition to diagrams and cover almost all radios made from about 1930 to the late 1950s. They take up space but are useful if you are going to do a lot of work. Except for volumes 1, 2, 3, and 23, they can be bought for a quite reasonable cost, if you can find them.

Sams folders. Howard B. Sams began publishing folders from 1946 on. The company is still publishing service information today. Unfortunately its early material is out of print. These provide the most thorough information you can find, often better than the service information provided by the manufacturers.

It is hard to find the early Sams folders. Sometimes these are bound in volumes. My collection, which extends into the mid-1960s, is housed in 79 volumes, each $4\frac{1}{2}$ inches thick.

Most collectors won't want or need that much information. If you use your common sense, your knowledge of electronics, and the information in this book, you can service most of the old radios available. Still, it is useful to look for and purchase the professional literature when you can find it.

Other Books and Sources

Sometimes the old radio magazines (*Radio News* and *Radio Craft*, for example) can be found. They are both fascinating and useful. Many radio collectors seriously collect old magazines, advertising, and literature. I am one of those collectors.

There are many older books on radio the-
ory, amateur radio, and servicing. Look at the books in stock at used book stores and old radio specialty dealers. If they look like they might help you, buy and read! This is a low-priced way to expand your knowledge.

There are five books I especially recommend.

John Markus's *Television and Radio Repairing* (New York: McGraw-Hill, 1953) is elementary, focusing on the techniques of service more than on theory. Good drawings, many of them reused in this book, are provided.

Alfred Ghirardi and J. Richard Johnson's *Radio and Television Receiver Troubleshooting and Repair* (New York: Rinehart, 1952) is an excellent, systematic text on servicing, providing good instruction on technique and the theory behind it. If you can find it, get it. I think it is the best. Any of the Ghirardi books going back into the early 1930s are well done. Ghirardi's 1931 book *Radio Physics Course* (New York-Radio Technical Publishing Company) is a classic.

Abraham Markus's *Radio Servicing: Theory and Practice* (New York: Prentice-Hall, 1948) is good on theory. Markus wrote a number of books and is an excellent teacher.

Abraham Markus and William Markus's *Elements of Radio* (New York: Prentice Hall, 1943) originally was prepared for preinduction radio training. This book is a very fine source of basic electronics understanding.

William Wellman's *Elementary Radio Servicing* (New York: Van Nostrand, 1947) is a technical high school text using a job sheet approach. It is good on technique but not too good on theory.

At the time this book was first written, in 1982, only one book on servicing old tube-type radios was available: Clayton Hallmark's *How to Repair Old-Time Radios* (Blue Ridge Summit, Pa.: Tab Books, 1979). Still a good text, it has been joined by many other books for repairers and restorers. I will not try to identify or recommend all of the new books in this growing field. Check on what is available since books on radios often go out of print.

Read all you can and practice what you read. If you find some new ideas on troubleshooting, try them out. You will learn and develop your own style.

Zenith 1948 model 5E01 ivory plastic five-tube AC/DC AM radio.

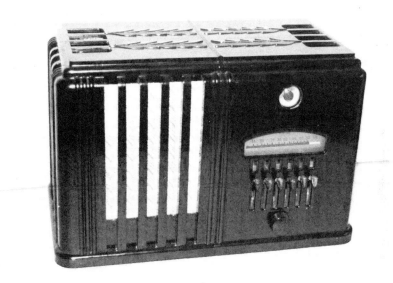

Airline 1937 radio in brown Bakelite case with leaf design in relief on the top.

Zenith 1946 model D6015 brown Bakelite radio. Although it is portable (note the handle), it operates only on AC current.

Sources for Parts

Many people supply parts for repair and restoration. Many of the supplies you need will be found at your local Radio Shack store. A useful general source of parts and tubes is Antique Electronics Supply, 6221 South Maple Avenue, Tempe, AZ 85283. A reliable source for test equipment and some supplies is Fordham Radio, 260 Motor Parkway, Hauppauge, NY 11788.

Many specialty suppliers and individuals have made reproductions of some of the most difficult-to-get parts for some major brands. I do not want to exclude worthy sources, but I could never list them all. Read at least one national magazine on collecting and join an antique radio collector club near you. These are the places where you will find the information you need.

Sources for Information

Two information sources come to mind that have been around for many years: *Antique Radio Classified* (P.O. Box 2, Carlisle, MA 01741) and *Radio Age* (636 Cambridge Road, Augusta, GA 30909). Both carry interesting articles, extensive adds, and information about the many clubs that have sprung up across the country. Write one or both of these magazines for subscription information. Either one will keep you up to date.

There are many clubs, so look for one close to you. Two national clubs stand out and publish excellent magazines: Antique Wireless Association (Box E, Breesport, NY 14816) and Antique Radio Club of America (3445 Adaline Drive, Stow, OH 44224).

Appendix: Information on Common Tubes

Basic information on some common tubes is helpful when you are testing filaments or identifying pins on a tube socket for voltage tests or reconstructing a circuit. These diagrams show the numbering of the pins, looking at them from the bottom of the tube. When you get an opportunity, buy an old tube manual, as it will give you much useful information. RCA tube manuals are the most useful and common. For more information on tube operation see Chapter 2 and the sections on circuit operation.

Tube pins are marked on the diagrams with the following letter identifications: F = filament; G (or G1) = control grid; H = heater; P = plate; HL = heater tap for panel lamp; K = cathode; NC = no connection; G2 = screen grid; PD = diode plate.

Tube identifiers. Later tubes with octal bases used an identifying system consisting of a number, one or more letters, and a number. Sometimes in reading circuit diagrams, you will find that one or more letters follow the last number, for example, 6F6, 6F6G, 6F6GT. All three are power output tubes of the pentode type. The 6F6 is a metal shell tube, the 6F6G is a glass tube with a large shell, and the 6F6GT is a glass tube with a smaller tubular shell. These usually are interchangeable. Sometimes, in R.F. amplification or mixer use, the metal tube with its built-in shielding will work where a glass one will not. The glass tube would be all right if it had an outside metal shield attached.

Old tube identifiers. Tubes like '01A, '12A,

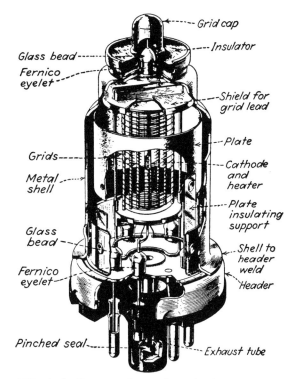

FIG. A–1 *Cutaway picture of metal tube.*

and '71A usually are identified on the tube and in diagrams with a 1, 2, or 3 leading number—for example, 101A, 201A, and 301A. The first number refers to the manufacturer and has nothing to do with the tube's characteristics. The 1, 2, and 3 tubes are inter-

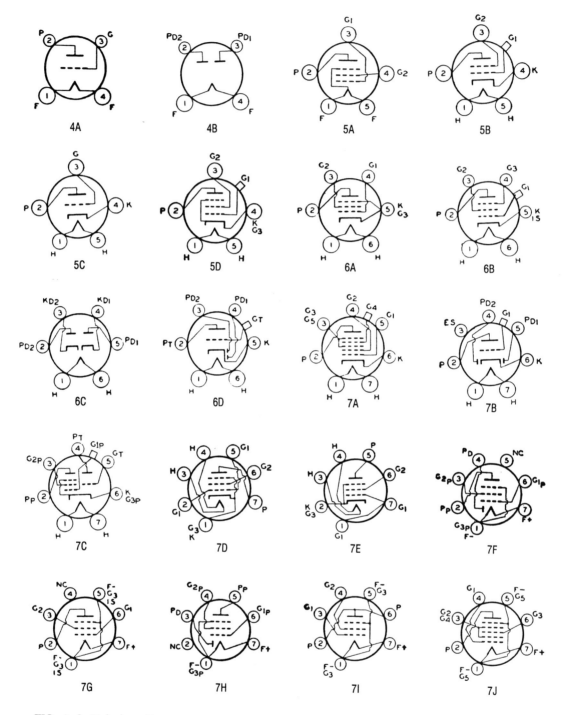

FIG. A–2 *Tube base diagrams.*

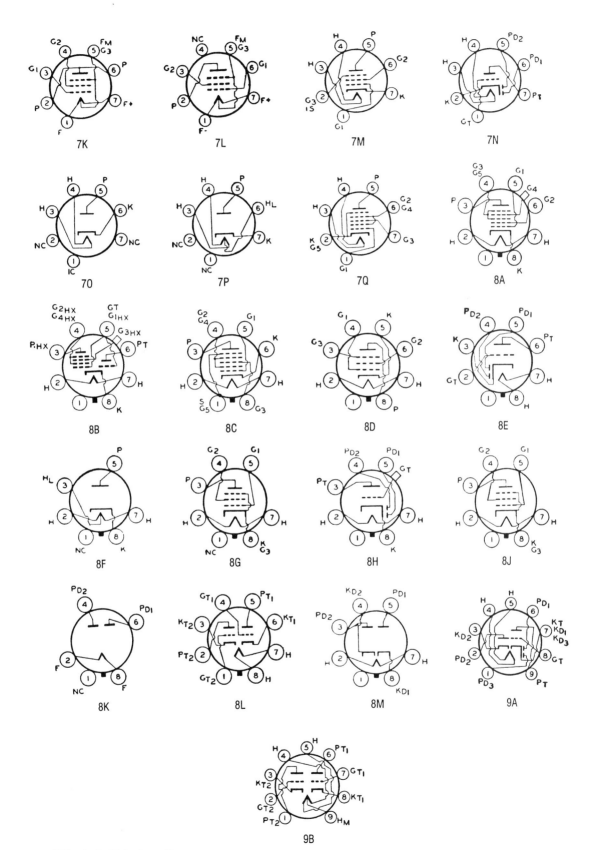

FIG. A-3 *Tube base diagrams.*

Tube Number	Base #	Fil. Volts	Plate Volts Max.	Type of Tube	Use in Circuit
'01A	4A	5v	135v	triode	general amplifier
1R5	7J	1.4v	90v	pentagrid	converter
1S4	7I	1.4v	67.5v	pentode	power output
1S5	7H	1.4v	90v	diode-pentode	detector, amplifier
1T4	7G	1.4v	90v	pentode	R.F. amplifier
1U4	7G	1.4v	110v	pentode	R.F. amplifier
1U5	7F	1.4v	90v	diode-pentode	detector
2A5	6A	2.5v	375v	pentode	power output
3Q4	7K	2.8v	90v	pentode	power output
3S4	7K	2.8v	90v	pentode	power output
3V4	7L	2.8v	90v	pentode	power output
5Y3	8k	5v		double diode	power supply rectifier
6A7	7A	6.3v	300v	pentagrid	converter
6A8	8A	6.3v	300v	pentagrid	converter
6C6	6B	6.3v	300v	pentode	R.F. amplifier
6C7	7B	6.3v	250v	dual diode-triode	detector, audio amplifier
6D6	6B	6.3v	300v	pentode	R.F. amplifier
6F6	8J	6.3v	375v	pentode	power output
6F7	7C	6.3v	250v	triode-pentode	general purpose
6H6	8M	6.3v		dual diode	detector
6K6	8J	6.3v	315v	pentode	power output
6K8	8B	6.3v	300v	triode-hexode	amplifier, converter
6Q7	8H	6.3v	300v	dual diode-triode	detector, audio amplifier
6SA7	8C	6.3v	300v	penagrid	converter
6SK7	8D	6.3v	300v	pentode	R.F. amplifier
6SN7	8L	6.3v	300v	dual triode	general amplifier
6SQ7	8E	6.3v	300v	dual diode-triode	detector, audio amplifier
6V6	8J	6.3v	315v	pentode	power output
'12A	4A	5v	180v	triode	power output
12AT6	7N	12.6v	300v	dual diode-triode	detector, audio amplifier
12AT7	9B	12.6v	300v	dual diode	amplifier, converter
12AU6	7M	12.6v	300v	pentode	R.F. amplifier
12AU7	9B	12.6v	300v	dual triode	general amplifier
12AV6	7N	12.6v	300v	dual diode-triode	detector, audio amplifier
12AX7	9B	12.6v	300v	dual triode	general amplifier
12BA6	7M	12.6v	300v	pentode	R.F. amplifier
12BE6	7Q	12.6	300v	pentagrid	converter
12SA7	8C	12.6v	300v	pentagrid	converter
12SK7	8D	12.6v	300v	pentode	R.F. amplifier
12SQ7	8E	12.6v	300v	dual diode-triode	detector, audio amplifier
19T8	9A	18.9v	300v	triple diode-triode	FM/AM detector, audio amp
24A	5B	2.5v	250v	pentode	R.F. amplifier
25L6	8G	25v	200v	beam power	power output
25Z5	6C	25v		double diode	rectifier in power supply
26	4A	1.5v	180v	triode	general amplifier
27	5C	2.5v	275v	triode	general amplifier
30	4A	2v	180v	triode	amplifier, detector
35B5	7E	35v	117v	beam power	power output
35C5	7D	35v	135v	beam power	power output
35L6	8G	35v	200v	beam power	power output
35W4	7P	35v		diode	rectifier in power supply
35Z5	8F	35v		diode	rectifier in power supply
36	5B	6.3v	250v	tetrode	R.F. amplifier

Tube Number	Base #	Fil. Volts	Plate Volts Max.	Type of Tube	Use in Circuit
39/44	5D	6.3v	250v	pentode	R.F. amplifier
41	6A	6.3v	315v	pentode	power output
42	6A	6.3v	375v	pentode	power output
43	6A	25v	160v	pentode	power output
45	4A	2.5v	275v	triode	power output
47	5A	2.5v	250v	pentode	power output
50B5	7E	50v	135v	beam power	power output
50C5	7D	50v	135v	beam power	power output
50L6	8G	50v	200v	beam power	power output
56	5C	2.5v	250v	triode	general amplifier
57	6B	2.5v	300v	pentode	audio amplifier
58	6B	2.5v	300v	pentode	R.F. amplifier
'71A	4A	5v	180v	triode	power output
75	6D	6.3v	250v	dual diode-triode	detector, audio amplifier
76	5C	6.3v	250v	triode	general amplifier
77	6B	6.3v	300v	pentode	amplifier, detector
78	6B	6.3v	300v	pentode	R.F. amplifier
80	4B	5v		double diode	rectifier in power supply
89	6B	6.3v	180v	pentode	power output
117Z3	7O	117v		diode	rectifier in power supply

changeable. In some literature, a tube will be identified as '01A or simply 01A.

Purchasing replacement tubes. Before buying a replacement tube, check the prices of two or more sources, if possible. Tubes can cost four times as much from one source to another, so it pays to shop around. If you can test tubes, save good ones from junked sets. For most use, tubes that test 75 percent of new value are usable.

⫸⫸⫸⫸⫸⫸ Glossary

A: heater or filament voltage for a tube. Supplied by battery or power supply.

AC (alternating current): type of current in which the direction of the electron flow changes regularly at a rate measured in cycles per second, or hertz (Fig. G–1).

AC-DC: a radio capable of operating from either an AC or a DC primary power source.

Aerial: a conductor or system of conductors used for radiating or receiving radio waves.

Alignment: the adjustment of receiver internal controls for the best reception of signals.

Ampere (amp): the unit of current flow. The current through a resistance of one ohm at an electrical pressure of one volt.

Amplification: the increase in the voltage, current, or power of a signal.

Antenna: aerial.

Arcing: electron current across a gap between two conductors.

Audio frequency (A.F.): an audible frequency, about 20 to 20,000 cycles (hertz) per second.

Audion: the vacuum tube developed by Lee DeForest.

Automatic volume control (AVC): a method of maintaining the output volume of a re-

ceiver at a constant level, regardless of variations in the R.F. input signal strength.

B (B+): the positive plate voltage used to draw electrons emitted by the cathode or filament to produce a useful current through a tube. It is supplied by battery or power supply.

Bakelite: trade name for a phenolic plastic used for insulation.

B eliminator: A-B voltage power supply getting its energy from an AC power source.

Bias: a negative voltage applied between the grid and cathode of a tube to reduce current through the tube to a desired level.

Blocking condenser: a condenser used to keep direct current out of a circuit while passing alternating current.

Breakdown voltage: the voltage at which an insulator or dielectric will puncture, causing an electric arc and failure of the part.

Broadcasting: transmission of speech or music to a broad audience by means of radio frequency waves.

Bypass condenser: a condenser used to provide an alternating current path around some circuit element.

C: negative voltage, called bias, applied between the grid of a tube and its cathode. Allows a tube to operate more accurately as an amplifier.

Cable: several insulated wires within an outer covering.

Capacitor: a condenser. A device used to store small amounts of electrical energy. It will pass changes in charge level while resisting unchanging energy movement.

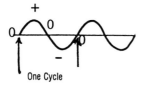

FIG. G–1 *AC cycle.*

Carrier wave: the radio frequency output of a transmitter that may or may not be modulated by a signal.

Carrier frequency: the frequency of a transmitter's carrier wave.

Cathode: source of electron flow in a vacuum tube.

Center tap: the mechanical and electrical center of a transformer winding or a resistor.

Charge: the condition of having an excess or absence of electrons.

Chassis: the base (usually metal) on which a radio is built.

Choke coil: a coil having high inductance, which opposes alternating current while allowing passage of direct current.

Coil: a wire wound in a circular form that possesses inductance.

Component: a part of a circuit. (Examples: condenser, resistor, transformer, tube, speaker, tube socket, and so on.)

Condenser: a capacitor. Two conducting surfaces (plates) separated by an insulator (dielectric). If one plate receives a charge, the other plate will develop an opposite charge. Changing charges on one plate will cause a corresponding change on the other. Steady charges, such as a DC voltage, will charge the opposite plate only once. No steady current will flow, but a varying current will.

Condenser capacity: the electrostatic storage ability of a condenser, measured in farads.

Condenser leakage: a small flow of current through a condenser with a faulty dielectric.

Conductor: a material that allows current to flow through it easily when a voltage is applied between its ends.

Contact points: the metal parts of a switch that complete a circuit when they touch.

Converter: in superheterodyne radio this is the stage that converts the desired incoming radio frequency signal into a lower intermediate frequency signal.

Crystal detector: a detector that operates through the rectifying qualities of certain minerals.

Current: electron flow.

Cycle: one complete positive and one complete negative alternation of an alternating current. Measured in cycles per second or hertz. See Fig. G-1.

DC (direct current): an electrical current in which the flow of electrons is always in one direction.

Demodulation: the process of detection of a modulated wave, current, or voltage, in order to obtain the signal given it in the modulation process.

Detector (demodulator): device removing the radio frequency part of a signal, leaving its audio portion.

Dielectric: a nonconducting medium. Any insulation between two conductors permitting electrostatic attraction and repulsion to take place across it.

Diode: a two-element device, usually a vacuum tube or crystal, that rectifies a current. It acts as a valve allowing current to flow in one direction only.

Distortion: an unfaithful reproduction of the original waveform of a signal.

Dry cell: a chemical cell producing 1.5 volts.

Dynamic loudspeaker: a moving coil loudspeaker.

Electric circuit: a complete conductive path permitting electron flow (Fig. G-2).

Electrolytic condenser: a condenser in which the electrolyte and an electrode serve as plates. The dielectric is a film formed by electrolysis. The condenser has a high capacity and is used for power supply filter and audio frequency bypass.

Electron: the negative portion of an atom. The moving portion of an electric current.

Element: one of the electrodes (working parts) of a tube or other device.

Emission: electron release from a heated cathode or filament.

Farad: the unit of measurement of capacity.

Feedback: the transfer of energy from the output to the input of the same circuit.

Field: the effect of an electrical current or a magnetic source on the space surrounding it.

Field coil: the magnetic coil producing the

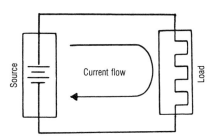

FIG. G–2 *Electrical circuit (source and load).*

magnetic force in a type of dynamic speaker.

Filament: a directly heated electron emitter in a vacuum tube.

Filament circuit: all parts through which filament heating current flows.

Filament rheostat: a variable resistance used to regulate the voltage to the filament of a tube. In some old sets it is used for volume control.

Filter choke: an inductance used in a power supply to filter out DC variations (ripple).

Filter condenser: the condenser used in a filter system to pass alternating or ripple currents to ground while keeping the direct current (B+) in the circuit.

First detector: in a superheterodyne receiver, the tube in which the received signal is mixed with a signal generated in the set to form an intermediate frequency. Sometimes called a converter.

Frequency: the number of cycles per second of an alternating current.

Front panel: the surface on which most working controls for a receiver are placed.

Full wave rectifier: a two-section rectifier, arranged so current is allowed to pass to the load in the same direction during each half-cycle of the AC supply. One part works during one-half cycle, and the other during the next.

Fuse: a protective device that will break the circuit if excessive current flows within it.

Gain: the ratio of the output to the input of an amplifier, power, current, or voltage.

Gang condenser: two or more variable condensers operating from one control shaft.

Grid: a wire coil or screen between the cathode and plate of a tube. When charged it retards or aids the flow of electrons from that cathode to the plate.

Grid circuit: the grid and cathode of a tube, together with all parts connecting them.

Grid current detection: the signal rectified in the grid circuit. Grid current flows through a high resistance, varying the bias on the tube at the modulation frequency. The tube amplifies the bias change.

Grid leak: a resistance in the grid circuit of a tube that permits excess electrons to leak off the grid after each charge. Electrons accumulating on the grid would eventually block the tube, preventing operation.

Grid leak detector: a tube accomplishing grid current detection.

Ground: the earth and all parts of a circuit connected directly to it.

Ground Fault Interrupter (GFI): a device to shut off an electrical circuit if current flows outside of the path it is designed to control.

Heater: the electric heater that heats the cathode of a tube, allowing the cathode to emit electrons.

Henry (H): the unit of electrical inductance.

Hertz (Hz): a unit of frequency equal to one cycle per second.

Heterodyne: the combination of two separate frequencies.

Hum: low-pitched droning sound produced by a line frequency signal that has entered an audio amplifier.

Impedance: the total opposition of a circuit to alternating current, due to resistance and reactance. Measured in ohms.

Inductance: character of a circuit opposing any change in current flow. Measured in Henrys (H).

Inductive reactance: the opposition of a pure inductance to the flow of alternating current. Measured in ohms.

Inductor: a coil.

Input: the point at which power is put into a device, or the power that is introduced.

Insulation: material used to prevent the flow of current between conductors.

Interference: any undesired noise or signal entering a receiver.

Intermediate frequency (I.F.): the frequency produced by combining a locally generated signal and the desired carrier signal it receives. In superheterodyne receivers, this provides a new signal frequency that can be better amplified and tuned, improving reception.

Intermittent: an irregular or occasional contact or connection within a circuit caused by shorting, loose connections, or other faults.

Interstage transformer: a transformer used to couple two vacuum tube stages together.

Isolation transformer: a transformer with an equal number of primary and secondary turns. It is used to isolate the incoming line from equipment connected to it. See Fig. G–3.

Kilocycle (kc): 1,000 cycles per second.

Kilohertz (kHz): kilocycle.

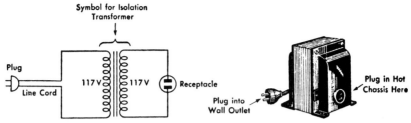

FIG. G–3 *Isolation transformer (from Markus)*.

Lead: a conductor attached to an electrical device.

Lead-in: connection between antenna and receiver.

Line: a conductor supplying current to a load some distance from its source.

Load: place where electron flow does work (see Fig. G–2).

Local oscillations: any oscillating currents generated in a receiver.

Loop antenna: an antenna of continuous turns of wire on a supporting frame (Fig. G–4).

Loudspeaker: a device for converting audio frequency current into sound waves.

Magnetic field: the field produced in the vicinity of a magnet.

Megahertz (mHz): a unit of frequency equal to 1 million hertz.

Mica condenser: a high-quality condenser with mica dielectric.

Microfarad (mfd): a useful unit of capacity in radio work, which is $\frac{1}{1,000,000}$ of a farad. A micromicrofarad (mmfd) is $\frac{1}{1,000,000}$ of a microfarad.

Microphonic: condition existing when mechanical vibrations affect a tube, causing sounds in its output.

Milli-: prefix meaning one thousandth (1 milliamp $\frac{1}{1,000}$ or .001 ampere).

Mixer tube: a tube in which a locally generated frequency is combined with the carrier

FIG. G–4 *Loop antenna*.

signal frequency to obtain a desired intermediate frequency.

Modulated wave: a continuous wave, the amplitude or frequency of which is varied in accordance with the signal to be transmitted.

Motorboating: a low-frequency audio oscillation in an amplifier.

Multitester: a test meter capable of measuring a wide range of voltages, resistances, and currents.

Negative: any potential lower than another that is taken as a reference. Example: -6 volts is negative to -2 volts.

Neutralizing: the application of out-of-phase feedback to an amplifier to prevent oscillation.

Neutrodyne receiver: a receiver using neutralized tuned radio frequency amplifier stages.

Ohm: the unit of electrical resistance. The value of resistance permitting the flow of 1 ampere of current to 1 volt of pressure.

Ohmmeter: an instrument for measuring resistance, calibrated in ohms.

Ohm's law: defines the relationship of voltage (E), current (I), and resistance (R) in a circuit. Expressed as $I = E/R$.

Open: no electrical connection where one could or should exist.

Oscillating: alternately surging first in one direction and then in the reverse. Caused in a vacuum tube by feeding a portion of the output into its input.

Oscillating circuit: a circuit that contains inductance and capacity in which a voltage impulse produces a regularly reversing current.

Oscillator: a device for producing oscillating currents of a frequency determined by the physical constants of the circuit.

Oscilloscope: a device for displaying electrical phenomena on a cathode ray tube screen.

Output: power from a circuit sent to a load.

Output transformer: the iron core transformer coupling the power tube to a loudspeaker.

P.M. speaker: a dynamic speaker with a magnetic field produced by a strong permanent magnet. Used in most modern sets.

Paper condenser: a condenser using a paper dielectric.

Parallel circuit: a group of components through which power flows through individual, separate loads (Fig. G–5).

Pentode: a five-element vacuum tube.

Permanent magnet: a hardened piece of magnetized steel that will hold its magnetism indefinitely.

Plate: collector for electrons in a vacuum tube. Given positive charge to attract electrons.

Plate bypass condenser: a condenser in parallel with the load of a detector tube to bypass radio frequency currents to ground, leaving audio frequencies unchanged.

Plate circuit: the entire path through which a tube's plate current flows.

Plate condenser: a DC-blocking condenser in the plate circuit of a tube.

Plate current: the direct current flowing between the cathode and the plate of a tube.

Plate current detection: obtained by operating the detector with a high negative grid bias. As a result, the average plate current varies at the audio modulation frequency.

Plate voltage: the positive DC potential between the plate and cathode of a tube, called the B voltage.

Polarity: characteristic of a device that has or requires a certain positive or negative charge at certain points. Example: both batteries and electrolytic condensers have plus or minus poles.

Positive: a shortage of electrons with respect to earth or another part of a circuit.

Potential: the presence of electrons in excess or in fewer numbers than another point in a circuit produces an electrical pressure; called potential or voltage difference.

Potentiometer: a variable resistance voltage divider. Often used as a volume control.

Power amplifier: an amplifier designed to furnish power to a loudspeaker.

Power supply: a source for necessary operating voltages for a receiver. Sometimes called a battery eliminator, it receives its operating power from the AC power line.

Preselector: a device (usually a tuned circuit) placed ahead of a frequency converter to pass signals of desired frequency and to reduce all other frequencies.

Primary winding: the winding of a transformer to which power is applied.

Push pull amplification: two tubes used in such a way that each provides output during the half-cycle when the other is not amplifying or is operating out of phase.

Radiation: the transmission of energy in waveform through a medium. In the case of radio, space.

Radio frequency (R.F.): any frequency higher than about 50,000 cycles per second.

Radio frequency choke: an inductance coil offering a high opposition to radio frequency currents.

Radio frequency oscillator: a device that produces sustained oscillations at radio frequencies. It is usually in the form of a tuned circuit activated by a vacuum tube.

Radio frequency transformer: a transformer designed to operate at radio frequencies.

Radio spectrum: all frequencies capable of radiation.

Radio wave: an electromagnetic wave that travels through space.

Reactance: the opposition to the flow of alternating current by the inductance of a coil,

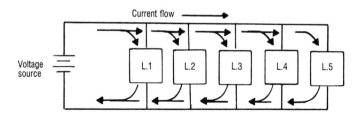

FIG. G–5 *Parallel circuit.*

the capacity of a condenser, or a combination of both.

Rectification: the process of producing direct current from alternating current.

Rectifier: a device that changes alternating current into pulsating direct current (Fig. G–6).

Reflex circuit: a circuit arrangement in which the signal is amplified, both before and after detection, in the same amplifier tubes.

Regeneration: increasing the energy input to a tube by feeding back part of the output into the input to be reamplified.

Regenerative detector: a vacuum tube detector in which regeneration is used to increase sensitivity by plate-to-grid coupling.

Resistance: the opposition to a flow of current. Measured in ohms.

Resistor: a unit offering a definite electrical resistance.

Resonance: the condition existing when the capacitive reactance and the inductive reactance are in exact opposition.

Resonant frequency: the frequency at which the inductive and capacitive reactance in a circuit become equal and cancel each other.

Rheostat: a variable resistance.

Screen grid: a grid placed between the control grid and the plate of a tube. Reduces tendency of tube to oscillate.

Second detector: the tube that detects the intermediate frequency in a superheterodyne receiver.

Secondary circuit: a circuit obtaining its energy by induction from another circuit.

Selectivity: the ability of a receiver to tune to a particular frequency while rejecting others.

Sensitivity: the degree to which a receiver responds to a given signal.

Series circuit: several loads arranged so that power flows through each in turn (Fig. G–7).

Sharp tuning: having a high degree of selectivity.

Shield: a conducting metal enclosure, attached to circuit ground, used to protect a circuit from the effects of external magnetic or electrical fields.

Short circuit (short): direct electrical connection where none should exist.

Short wave: generally, frequencies higher than 3,000 kilocycles.

Signal generator: a device that supplies a standard voltage of known amplitude, frequency, and waveform for measuring and test purposes.

Source: location of the origin of an electrical current or signal. See Fig. G–2.

Stage: a tube and its associated parts affecting a signal passing through it.

Superheterodyne receiver: a receiver in which the transmitted signal is mixed with a signal generated in the receiver, producing an intermediate frequency that is always the same. This intermediate frequency is amplified, tuned, and detected to reproduce the original audio frequency.

Switch: a device for changing the connections of a circuit.

Tetrode: a four-element tube.

Tickler coil: a winding used to couple the plate circuit of a tube with its grid circuit in a regenerative detector.

Tone control: any method of emphasizing either high or low tones at will.

Transformer: two or more windings with a common magnetic circuit, allowing the

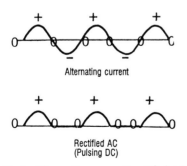

FIG. G–6 *Alternating current/rectified AC (pulsing DC).*

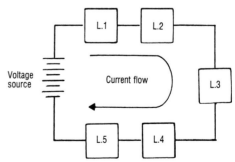

FIG. G–7 *Series circuit.*

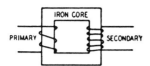

FIG. G–8 *Basic transformer.*

transfer of power by magnetic induction. Used to transfer power, increasing or decreasing its voltage, between two circuits. See Fig. G–8.

Trimmer condenser: a small, adjustable condenser in parallel with a tuning condenser or coil for aligning a tuned circuit with other circuits in a receiver.

Triode: a tube with three working elements.

Troubleshooting: to look for, locate, and repair malfunctioning equipment.

Tuned circuit: a circuit with parts selected to resonate at a certain frequency. That frequency may be reinforced, selected (and others rejected), or reduced in strength (trapped), depending on how the circuit is used.

Tuned radio frequency amplification (T.R.F.): amplification of radio frequency signal with coupling between stages provided by air core transformers with secondary windings tuned to resonate with the incoming radio frequency by tuning condensers.

Tuning: adjusting a circuit by varying its inductance or capacity to select a certain desired frequency while rejecting all other frequencies. The circuit is made to resonate at the desired frequency.

Tuning coil: an inductance coil in a circuit that may be tuned to resonance by varying its inductance.

Tuning condenser: a variable capacity condenser having one or more sets of fixed plates and one or more sets of rotating plates. It is adjusted to resonate with a fixed inductance at the desired frequency.

Vacuum tube: a device consisting of a number of electrodes contained within a high-vacuum enclosure.

Variable condenser: any condenser whose capacity can be changed during operation.

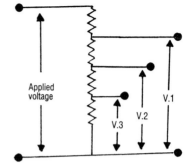

FIG. G–9 *Voltage divider.*

Vernier dial: a device by which a complete turn of the control knob turns a shaft only part of a turn.

Voice coil: a light coil attached to the cone of a dynamic speaker. The signal voltage in the coil reacts to the strong magnetic field surrounding it, moving the cone in proportion to the audio frequency voltage applied to it.

Volt (v or V): the practical unit of electrical force. The electrical pressure that will cause one ampere of current to flow through a resistance of one ohm.

Voltage divider: a series of resistances between a positive and negative source that separates certain lower voltages (v 1, v 2, v 3 in Fig. G–9) for a receiver.

Voltage drop: the difference between voltages at two points in a circuit.

Voltage rating: the maximum regular voltage at which a device may be operated without damage.

Voltmeter: an instrument that measures the voltage between two points.

Volume: the degree of loudness of sound produced by a loudspeaker.

Volume control: a device for regulating the intensity of volume.

Watt: the unit of electrical power equal to a current of one amp at a pressure of one volt.

Wavelength: the distance between two successive peaks of the same polarity on a wave. Usually measured in meters.

Winding: the wire forming a coil.

Wire-wound resistor: resistance wire-wound on an insulating form.

Index ⚜⚜⚜⚜⚜⚜⚜

repairing, 77, 80–81, 83
troubleshooting and, 54, 59, 62
Loudspeaker tester, 116

Magazines, 122, 124
Magnet, 15, 38
Magnetic flux, 15, 17
Magnetic force field, 15, 17
Magnetic generation, 15
Magnetism, 15, 17
Maintaining antique radios, 88, 90
Mass-market radio, 3, 6
Meissner 5 tube model 10–1191A, 102
Mica condenser, 35
Microfarad, 18
Micromicrofarad, 18
Mineral spirits, 91
Modification, 53
Motorboating, 50, 57
Mouse damage, 6
Multigrid converter tube, 24
Multitester, 49, 54, 114–115

Naphtha, 31
Negatively charged body, 14
Newsletters, 126
Nucleus, 14
Nut driver set, 113

Ohm, 14–15, 43, 65
Ohmmeter, 75
Open-contact tone, band, or phono switches, 40
Oscillation, 24
Oscilloscope, 117
Output transformer, 68–69, 106
Output tube, 68–69
Overheating, 48

Paintbrush, soft, 28, 113
Paper condenser, 34–35, 74–75
Paper veneer, 93
Parts of antique radios. *See also* specific names of
burns and, 45
changing, 45
cleaning, 31
diagrams of, 24
failure of, 54
fire hazard and, 45
missing, 6, 9
removing, 119, 121
replacing, 40
sources for, 126
substitute, 119
total restoration and, 5
Paste wax, 90
Paste wood filler, 96

Pentode amplifier, 105
Pentode tube, 24, 69, 71
Plastic cabinet, 6, 9, 100–101
Plates, 18, 21, 32
Playing antique radios
AC/DC sets, 49
AC sets, 48
battery sets, 48
first time for, 48–49
listening and, 49–50
safety precautions for, 28
voltage for, correct, 48, 49
Pliers, 113
Polarity, 15, 17
Portable radio, 3
Positively charged body, 14
Postwar radio, 6
Power pack, 6
Power resistor, 45
Power supply
AC/DC set, 6
AC set, 6, 49
battery, 6
circuit, 102, 104
fire hazard and, 45
operating, 48–49
overheating of, 49
protecting, 48
receiver theory, 102, 104
rectifier tube in, 21
repairing, 63–65
safety precautions, 49, 63
testing, 63–65
Power supply tester, 117
Practical restoration, 53
Preselector tuning, 104
Price, 13
Price guide, 3
Primitive radio, 3
Problems. *See* Troubleshooting; Veneer problems
Protective goggles, 47, 93
Proton, 14
Putt-putt sounds, 50

R (resistance), 14–15, 43, 63, 65
Radio. *See* Antique radio
Radio Age, 126
*Radio and Television Receiver Troubleshooting and
Repair* (Ghirardi and Johnson), 124
Radio Craft, 124
Radio frequency (R.F.)
amplifier, 26, 54, 69, 71
carrier, 24, 26
coils, 36–37
rates of, 15
receiving and, 26–27